theatre & nation

Theatre&
Series Editors: Jen Harvie and Dan Rebellato

Theatre&
Series Standing Order: ISBN 978–0–230–20327–3 paperback

You can receive further titles in this series as they are published by placing a standing order. Please contact your bookseller or, in the case of difficulty, write to us at the address below with your name and address, the title of the series, and the ISBN quoted above.

Customer Services Department, Palgrave Macmillan Ltd.
Houndmills, Basingstoke, Hampshire, RG21 6XS, England

theatre &
nation

Nadine Holdsworth

palgrave
macmillan

First published 2010 by
PALGRAVE MACMILLAN

Palgrave Macmillan in the UK is an imprint of Macmillan Publishers Limited, registered in England, company number 785998, of Houndmills, Basingstoke, Hampshire RG21 6XS.

Palgrave Macmillan in the US is a division of St Martin's Press LLC, 175 Fifth Avenue, New York, NY 10010.

Palgrave Macmillan is the global academic imprint of the above companies and has companies and representatives throughout the world.

Palgrave® and Macmillan® are registered trademarks in the United States, the United Kingdom, Europe and other countries.

ISBN 978-0-230-21871-0   paperback

This book is printed on paper suitable for recycling and made from fully managed and sustained forest sources. Logging, pulping and manufacturing processes are expected to conform to the environmental regulations of the country of origin.

A catalogue record for this book is available from the British Library.

A catalog record for this book is available from the Library of Congress.

Printed and bound in China

contents

series editors' preface

The theatre is everywhere, from entertainment districts to the fringes, from the rituals of government to the ceremony of the courtroom, from the spectacle of the sporting arena to the theatres of war. Across these many forms stretches a theatrical continuum through which cultures both assert and question themselves.

Theatre has been around for thousands of years, and the ways we study it have changed decisively. It's no longer enough to limit our attention to the canon of Western dramatic literature. Theatre has taken its place within a broad spectrum of performance, connecting it with the wider forces of ritual and revolt that thread through so many spheres of human culture. In turn, this has helped make connections across disciplines; over the past fifty years, theatre and performance have been deployed as key metaphors and practices with which to rethink gender, economics, war, language, the fine arts, culture and one's sense of self.

Theatre & is a long series of short books which hopes to capture the restless interdisciplinary energy of theatre and performance. Each book explores connections between theatre and some aspect of the wider world, asking how the theatre might illuminate the world and how the world might illuminate the theatre. Each book is written by a leading theatre scholar and represents the cutting edge of critical thinking in the discipline.

We have been mindful, however, that the philosophical and theoretical complexity of much contemporary academic writing can act as a barrier to a wider readership. A key aim for these books is that they should all be readable in one sitting by anyone with a curiosity about the subject. The books are challenging, pugnacious, visionary sometimes and, above all, clear. We hope you enjoy them.

Jen Harvie and Dan Rebellato

foreword

The first show I produced when I became Director of the National Theatre in April 2003 was Shakespeare's *Henry V*. When I scheduled it (in the summer of 2002) we had just fought a war in Afghanistan and it seemed likely that we would soon be fighting another in Iraq. It felt like exactly the play the National Theatre should be doing: it has often been a barometer of public opinion in times of war, and as it turned out the Iraq war started during rehearsals.

It would have been perverse not to present it as a contemporary state-of-the-nation play, and I'm not sure that the audience would have allowed us any other approach. One small example from the very start of the play: the King needs rock-solid justification in law for the invasion of France – an action recommended by his dying father 'to busy giddy minds / With foreign quarrels'. The Archbishop of Canterbury obliges him, before his Council, at great length. At the National in 2003 he handed copies of an elaborately produced dossier round the cabinet table and referred to it repeatedly as he explained England's right under Salic law to take military action. The audience, force-fed by news media on dodgy dossiers and the Attorney General's advice to the Prime Minister, caught on instantly. The scene made concrete a sense of historical continuity: war leaders have always gone to great lengths to massage the case for war, and the South Bank of the Thames, in 1599 as in 2003, was the place people gathered to work out what they felt about it.

So eager was the National Theatre's audience to see contemporary history in Shakespeare's history play that there was a significant loss. There is a characteristically Shakespearean ambiguity about Henry V: he may be ruthless and out for himself, but he's also the heroic embodiment of the kind of nation-builder that has only recently fallen out of favour. A production less at the mercy of current events would have given theatrical presence to his heroism, and his rhetoric might have seemed less manipulative, more inspirational. But Henry was tainted by his association with Tony Blair. The resemblance is only superficial, but the audience wanted too badly to discuss the kind of leader they thought Blair was. They were never more attentive than when the King – as he often does – conflates his own agenda with the nation's, always alert to the tension in the play between the King's interests and those of the common man.

Nadine Holdsworth's excellent book offers a persuasive overview of the ways nation and national identity have been present in a whole range of theatrical practices, and it would be instructive to apply her findings to productions of *Henry V* throughout the 400 years that have passed since its first performance in 1599 at the Globe. For a theatre producer it is always bracing to be required to think theoretically about the purpose of playing. There is always the temptation to think only about what might fill the house tomorrow. It's impossible to know what exactly impelled Shakespeare to write his two best state-of-the-nation plays, *Henry IV Parts 1* and *2*. But we can be pretty sure why his company must have wanted the sequel. Agincourt was box-office gold, and Shakespeare's was the fourth *Henry V* play to open in ten years. Part of the reason we did it at the National in 2003 was that we thought it would sell seats. We've gone on to commission and produce large-scale plays in the Olivier and Lyttelton Theatres by writers such as David Eldridge, Richard Bean, Moira Buffini and David Hare, as much as anything because we sniffed in the audience a real appetite for contemporary reflections of national identity and national crisis on our larger stages. This book should provoke a myriad of new ways to think about them.

Nicholas Hytner is Director of the National Theatre.

theatre & nation

Britain's Got Talent and national conviviality

As I write, the televised talent contest *Britain's Got Talent* is reaching its conclusion for 2009. The influential cultural critic Homi Bhabha, in his 1990 *Nation and Narration*, theorises that the way a nation sees itself and projects itself to others is tied up in the narratives a nation tells itself about itself, including both the 'what' and the 'how' of the telling (p. 3), and I think this is an interesting way of approaching this popular cultural format. Created by the *X-Factor* and *Pop Idol* originator, Simon Cowell, 'Got Talent' has become a global phenomenon since 2006, with franchises in the United States, India, South Africa, New Zealand, the Philippines, and many countries across Europe and South America. Each of these franchises provides a site for live performances by singers, dance troupes, circus acts, comedians and musicians that are transmitted to millions of homes nationally and internationally via television and global media networks.

But, importantly, unlike other global franchises such as McDonald's and Starbucks, which thrive on sameness and familiarity wherever they are, each version of 'Got Talent' is inflected through its national context in a way that underscores the persistence of a particular cultural image of the nation in an age of globalisation. So, in India, where the show first aired in 2009, the finalists included Aslan Khan, a traditional folk music group, and Mandeep Singh with his Bhangra Punjabi folk dance, while virtuoso circus acts such as Dmitry Bulkin, a twenty-two-year-old acrobat, have dominated the show in Russia.

At the same time, the 'Got Talent' brand provides a popular space that highlights the changing state and status of nations under the influence of new technologies, migration and globalisation.

In the British context, *Britain's Got Talent* exhibits and celebrates many of the values Britain likes to project about itself as a nation: patriotism, democracy and eccentricity, to name a few. In a 2005 article entitled 'You Crazy Rosbifs', the French author Catherine Poirier Agnès argued that 'the British are the kings of eccentricity. They practice it better than anyone else and it's not a passing thing. From George III to Boy George, by way of "Beau" Brummell, Oscar Wilde, Monty Python and Vivienne Westwood, their aristocratic pretensions to the art of eccentricity are beyond all compare'. Of *Britain's Got Talent*, Tim Walker writes, in 'Cowell's Reality Circus Espouses British Talent for Eccentricity' (2009), 'Eccentricity is our forte, and Britain's Got Talent celebrates it.' As farmers dance with wheelbarrows, a 73-year-old grandfather break-dances and a group of elderly women embark on extreme knitting as a spectator sport, it is hard to disagree with Agnès and Walker. Alongside the virtuoso singing performances are a host of British eccentrics claiming their fifteen minutes of fame with mad, bad and excruciating acts.

The patriotism inherent in the show functions on an explicit symbolic level. The title of the show asserts that Britain *has* got talent, and the 3,000-strong live audience are going to shout about it. The show's logo, with its prominent Union Jack flag, features on trailers, the stage backdrop and the website (www.talent.itv.com). The judges consistently praise the acts as evidence of Britain's brilliance and, alongside £100,000, the winner gets the opportunity to perform at the annual Royal Variety Performance, a show that receives lower ratings than *Britain's Got Talent* but gains prestige by its royal audience and longevity as a cultural institution. *Britain's Got Talent*'s blatant recourse to national iconographic figures and symbols frames the show as a quintessentially British product, but many other things destabilise the homogenising coherence of its visual onslaught, including the global response to the 2009 audition of Susan Boyle, an unassuming forty-seven-year-old unemployed Scottish charity worker.

Boyle's rendition of 'I Dreamed a Dream' from *Les Misérables* (Barbican theatre, London, 1985) immediately became a global Internet sensation through the power of YouTube. Within days of her audition, more than forty million people worldwide had seen the video clip of Boyle singing. She became the hot subject of discussion on the social networking site Twitter, where one message, quoted by Leigh Holmwood in 'Susan Boyle: A Dream Come True' (2009), claimed, 'And in the news today, stockmarkets surged to pre-Sept highs as Susan Boyle returns optimism and inspiration to the world over.' Journalists from around the world descended on Boyle's hometown, the *Washington Post* published a front-page story on her, and the American chat-show hosts Larry King and Oprah Winfrey interviewed Boyle for their shows. The triumph of an individual defying the expectations created by her initial appearance was a globally appealing story that, by the power of international communications systems, reached millions worldwide.

The profile of the acts voted into the final by the public also speaks volumes about the diverse, multicultural character of Britain and supports Paul Gilroy's assertion in *After Empire: Melancholia or Convivial Culture?* (2004) that there is a need to discover value in Britain's 'ability to live with alterity without becoming anxious, fearful, or violent' (p. xi). The winners of the 2009 contest, Diversity, an eleven-strong, multiracial, all-male street dance group aged twelve to twenty-five, epitomised Gilroy's optimistic call for a 'convivial culture', a far-cry from the tenor of his seminal *There Ain't No Black in the Union Jack* (1987), which brutally dissected the failure of Britain to embrace the presence of racial difference. Defining 'convivial culture' Gilroy refers to 'the processes of cohabitation and interaction that have made multi-culture an ordinary feature of social life in Britain's urban areas and in postcolonial cities elsewhere'

(p. ix). Gilroy is quick to point out that conviviality does not describe the end of racism or the triumph of tolerance. Indeed, the election of two far-right British National Party candidates to the European Parliament in June 2009 provides a salutary reminder of this fact. But when the judges confidently touted a young boy, Shaheen Jafargholi, as the Welsh successor to Tom Jones – the iconic Welsh singing sensation with the quintessentially Welsh name – it brought home how something in the state of the British nation has irrevocably altered.

Structure and scope of this book

After opening up these thoughts on the changing state and status of the nation through the popular cultural example of the *Got Talent* brand, I provide an overview of the various ways in which leading thinkers have conceived the terms *nation*, *nationalism* and *national identity* and offer some reflection on what I think are the strengths and weaknesses of their positions. These ideas provide a theoretical framework for my investigation of the theatre practices that subsequently come under scrutiny. It is important to state at this point that, although postcolonialism has been crucial to unlocking structures of power and the political, social and cultural mechanisms at the heart of numerous national contexts, I will not be engaging with postcolonial theory explicitly, although I will refer to some theatre practices that negotiate postcolonial situations. The area of theatre and postcolonialism is so extensive and complex that it deserves a book in its own right rather than being integrated into or overlaid on a short book that has the nation as its primary focus.

This book asks a fundamental question: What do we mean when we combine the term *theatre* with *nation*? On a basic level, we can think of theatre as something intrinsically connected to the nation because it enhances 'national' life by providing a space for shared civil discourse, entertainment, creativity, pleasure and intellectual stimulation. Theatre, as a material, social and cultural practice, offers the chance to explore national histories, behaviours, events and preoccupations in a creative, communal realm that opens up potential for reflection and debate. But it is more than this. Arguably, theatre is deeply implicated in constructing the nation through the imaginative realm and provides a site where the nation can be put under the microscope. For example, in South Africa theatre had a prominent role in highlighting the brutal injustices of the Apartheid era and provided a voice of dissent through organisations such as the Market Theatre of Johannesburg. And, since Apartheid's collapse, South African theatre has been under considerable pressure, as the playwright Mike van Graan has acknowledged (in Charles J. Fourie's 2006 volume *New South African Plays*), to 'concentrate on building the rainbow nation' (p. 172) through a focused approach to subject matter and representation that positively embrace the reconfigured national image.

I want to pursue a particular line of enquiry in this book. The core of my argument is that the vast majority of theatre practices that engage with the nation, directly or obliquely, do so to respond to moments of rupture, crisis or conflict. My argument, then, is that theatre often deploys its content, formal properties and aesthetic pleasures to generate a creative dialogue with tensions in the national fabric. Hence, I spend some time situating the emergence of state-sanctioned national theatres as sites for asserting political power and/or national cultural autonomy as a response to colonialism or as part of a postcolonial moment of re-imagining the nation. Similarly, I argue that the raison d'être of most state-of-the-nation plays is to explicitly critique the nation. I illustrate this argument with a detailed consideration of a range of theatre works that take a riot or series of riots as their stimulus to explore social breakdown and civic unrest in a manner that is complex and multi-dialogical. Continuing to focus my argument on how theatre and performance practices hold up nations for scrutiny and critique, I turn to the powerful role and function of national iconography. In particular, I am interested in how playwrights and theatre-makers ironically, satirically and creatively deploy national iconography to undermine and destabilise the homogeneous national image in their work. I argue that theatre opens up a creative space for exploring the paradoxes, ambiguities and complexities around issues of tradition, identity, authenticity and belonging associated with the nation.

The final part of my argument is rooted in a desire to locate theatre that captures the rich diversity and rampant eclecticism of nations as they shift and change through the impact of migration, globalisation and transnational exchange. I posit that, as we move through the twenty-first century, we could do worse than be mindful of Gilroy's notion of conviviality, and I begin to explore where we might find evidence of a cosmopolitan convivial theatre practice. I also offer some reflection on how the meanings associated with a convivial culture might be an integral component of theatre practices emerging from artists who embrace the *other* as part of the national *us* to question what we really mean when we think of the nation in theatre and theatre in the nation.

In line with the extension of what falls under the umbrella term 'theatre' since the avant-garde movements of the early twentieth century and the more recent influence of new media technologies, I will refer to plays but also delve into performance installations, public art projects and multimedia performances to illustrate my argument. I hope to draw attention to the fact that a national theatre not only appears at designated national theatres but comprises a complex nexus of theatrical activity, by looking at work that has appeared on main stages and at smaller-scale work by touring companies and artists who cross disciplinary boundaries. All my examples are drawn from the post-1945 period, and most from the recent past. I believe that theatre, despite its potential for universal resonances across time, often speaks most potently to the historical moment of its inception, and this relation is given prominence throughout the book. The theatre works I discuss are inevitably chosen and framed through my position as a Western, monoglot English-speaker, and so the majority of the works explored in this book originated in the United Kingdom, the United States or Australia. It would be fair to say that a completely different book on theatre and the nation would emerge from a writer coming from a non-Western perspective or with expertise in that field.

Before we look in detail at how the nation, national identity and nationalism have been manifest in a range of theatrical practices, it is important to distinguish what we mean by these terms.

Nation, national identity and nationalism

Throughout history people have constructed group formations to distinguish 'us' from 'them', whether territorial, linguistic or around bloodlines or religion, for example. In the contemporary world, nation is one of the most powerful of these markers of identity and belonging. Indeed, some of the most bitter and bloody conflicts of recent years have had their origins in campaigns for national expansion or national autonomy or in ideas about which ethnic group has the 'right' to occupy the nation. But it is important to be clear at the outset that there is simply no consensus on what nations are, what drives nationalism or how we should define national identity. So the following section introduces the work of a number of theorists and cultural critics who have undertaken a sustained consideration of the meaning and ramifications of these terms. The aim is to account for the multifaceted approaches to what constitutes the nation and nationalism as they inform our understanding of our place in the world, our sense of belonging and our identity as individuals. I explore the importance of various factors – such as history, territory, heredity, language and culture – to constructions of national identity and begin to identify the challenges to fixed ideas of nation and national identities posed by migration, multicultural communities and globalisation.

The nation as 'territorial community'

At its most basic level, the nation refers to a territorial community, so the borders that distinguish Italy from France, Switzerland, Austria and Slovenia define the nation, and people born within these borders are Italian citizens. But it is not as simple as this statement suggests. Very few nations have fixed territorial communities that stretch back through time. There are also instances of competing claims on the same territory, as in the ongoing crisis between Israelis and Palestinians in the Middle East. Nations are made and unmade by human beings; they are subject to historical forces and political change, including the redrawing of territorial boundaries or the break-up of nation-states. For example, in 2003, following the brutal Balkan conflict, Yugoslavia disappeared from the map of Europe, to be replaced by a number of smaller nations, including Bosnia-Herzegovina, Serbia and Montenegro, and Macedonia.

Historically, nations have used borders to limit the movement of people, goods and capital through mechanisms such as passports, border controls and trade agreements. There are even attempts to limit the transfer of ideas across national borders. For instance, China maintains strict control over the flow of information to its citizens by blocking access to several foreign news sites and the popular Internet search engine Google. Nonetheless, in a world dominated by the workings of a global economy, an increasingly international geopolitical environment and the networking of people through technology and transnational cultural exchange, national borders come under strain. Climate change, the global economic crisis, scientific discovery and swine flu sweeping across the world from its origins in South America all remind us that national borders are porous. Individual nations cannot remain impervious to or immune from events in other countries. This is no more evident than in the growing global diaspora of people traversing national borders as economic migrants, asylum-seekers and refugees. Despite all this, the nation has remained remarkably persistent as a political, social and economic force, and the following section identifies some of the reasons.

The nation and nationalism: where do they come from?

One view, described as *perennialism*, is that nations have always existed in one form or another and that it is possible to trace evidence of continuous national histories in several nations across the world. However, as Anthony D. Smith points out in his 2001 book *Nationalism*, this view rather conveniently sidesteps colonialism, global diasporas and historical discontinuities, which mean that 'a nation's identity and history may not reach back beyond the Renaissance or the late medieval epoch, as, for example, with Sweden,

Holland and Russia' (p. 50). Another term, *primordialism*, suggests that nations are a 'natural' phenomenon and the primary organising principle throughout the world – basically, nations are part of the natural order of things. This is problematic because its focus on the nation as an organic phenomenon could lead to essentialist forms of nationalism and an adherence to a belief that the will of the individual nation is paramount, rather than the more contemporary emphasis on transnational cooperation. Hence, at its extreme, primordialism could legitimate imperialist expansionist agendas or a refusal to cooperate in the global fight against climate change if cooperation went against a narrow definition of national interest.

Despite the general popularity of assuming that nations have long, unbroken histories, most theorists now recognise the nation as a relatively recent phenomenon. Since the mid-twentieth century, many theorists have subscribed to a *modernist* version of the nation that views it as originating in the specific economic, social and political material conditions of modernity, and industrialisation in particular. In this school of thought, the nation and nationality, according to David McCrone in *The Sociology of Nationalism* (1998), 'is not the result of sentiment or historical folk-memory; but is an essential part of the modern condition' (p. 68). The philosopher and sociologist Ernest Gellner is most associated with this position. A central plank of Gellner's contribution to the field is the idea that individuals who actively inhabit a national culture define the nation. In particular, Gellner stresses the modern phenomenon of public education systems that create individuals literate in the national language and how the language of the nation-state imbues them with nationalist tendencies. McCrone usefully refers to state education as functioning like 'state religion in secular form' (p. 71) in the way that it disseminates specific national ideologies.

Whereas Gellner highlights the mechanisms supporting industrialisation as a driving factor, theorists such as Tom Nairn emphasise how the forces of industrial capitalism, which creates regional inequalities and class divisions, mobilise people to support national sentiments and ideals. Connected to this idea is the Marxist historian Eric Hobsbawm's *constructionist* view that nations owe a great deal to invented traditions created to serve the interests of the ruling elite, to support imperial expansion and to channel the energies of the working population, who might otherwise unite to overthrow the capitalist system that exploits them. Other theorists, such as John Breuilly and Anthony Giddens, stress that the idea of the *modern professionalised state* provides the key to understanding how the nation is conceived and operates (see Smith, *Nationalism*, pp. 46–48). Thus, Breuilly argues in *Nationalism and the State* (1993) that nationalism is a vital component of the politics of the state in terms of legitimising autonomy, sovereignty and the loyalty of its citizenship.

These modernist approaches have significant limitations and omissions. They suggest that all citizens naturally gravitate towards and accept a singular national rhetoric and that there is a single national language to convey this. In a nation such as South Africa, which has eleven official languages and competing versions of the nation's history, culture and future, we might ask, How can *the* voice of the nation be adequately expressed? Equally, one of the consequences of modernity is the global movement of peoples, and this complicates Gellner's vision of education as a homogenising force because the reality for many is that the languages of their home and of their state are different. In addition, by locating nationalism as solely a product of the nation and modernity, the modernist approach overlooks the fact that nationalism emerges in many different socioeconomic contexts – rich and poor, developed and underdeveloped, preindustrial and industrial. As such, the modernist approach, in its stress on instrumentalism, does not explain how people relate to their nation on a deep emotional level of national consciousness and cultural sentiment.

Also, the modernist stance adheres to a rationalist, linear model of progressive history, but the history of many nations is such that old animosities and ethnic conflicts have a habit of resurfacing, as happened with such devastating consequences during the Balkan war. For these reasons, Anthony D. Smith insists on an *ethno-symbolic* approach, which asserts the centrality of pre-modern ethnic identities and communities to understanding the growth of nations and modern-day ethno-nationalisms. For Smith, nations are a demarcated territory, a shared political community with common institutions, laws, language and citizenship, but they are also activated through 'ethnic' elements such as common values, traditions and culture in the form of stories, myths, memories and histories. Steven Grosby uses the distinction between the words *house* and *home* as a way of understanding the significance of this relationship. In his 2005 book *Nationalism: A Very Short Introduction*, Grosby distinguishes between the nation as a 'house', a purely physical, spatial structure, and the nation as a 'home', 'where the "spirit" of past and current generations has filled up that spatial setting, making it a homeland, a territory' (p. 46). To delve fully into this distinction we need to rehearse the civic versus ethnic nationalism debate.

Civic versus ethnic nationalism

As we have seen, some definitions of nationalism emphasise observable factors, such as territory, laws and language, that are connected to the state; others put more stress on subjective elements, such as shared characteristics, attitudes and behaviours, associated with the people of a nation. In *The Idea of Nationalism*, first published in 1944, Hans Kohn categorised this division as 'Western' versus 'Eastern' nationalism. The former is seen as voluntary – people voluntarily subscribe to supporting the nation – whereas Eastern nationalism is organic, part of a bloodline that is inescapable. Kohn offers a simplistic, geographically driven dichotomy, but his work provided the foundation for many subsequent theories of nationalism. For instance, John Hutchinson refers to political versus cultural nationalism, and recently the contrasting terms 'civic' and 'ethnic' have become commonplace through the work of Smith.

Hutchinson argues that the civic and the ethnic forms of nationalism 'must not be conflated, for they articulate different, even competing conceptions of the nation, form their own distinctive organizations, and have sharply diverging political strategies' (John Hutchinson and Anthony D. Smith, *Nationalism*, 1994, p. 122). According to Hutchinson, civic nationalists such as Breuilly are primarily rationalists who see the nation as a territorial entity and are interested in how national citizens are equalised and united by common laws and institutions managed within the nation-state. This is problematic because civic nationalism, in its desire to assimilate all under the banner of the nation-state, fails adequately to endorse the rights of diverse cultural groups within society – spurring the 'Why can't they be more like us?' mentality. Ethnic nationalists, on the other hand, emphasise the uniqueness of ethnic groups established through a common history and a shared cultural heritage passed down through the generations in a literal and metaphorical bloodline. Thus, civic nationalists define nationality by birth within the territory of the nation, whereas ethnic nationalists define nationality on the basis of genealogy. This form of ethnic nationalism is highly problematic when it leads to attempts to reconstruct an ethnically diverse nation into a monocultural ethnic nation.

The twentieth and twenty-first centuries have witnessed a resurgence of ethnic nationalism dominated by the idea of a homeland for an ethnic group. In Nazi Germany, Hitler used a desire to secure the ethnic purity of the Aryan race to justify the extermination of millions of Jews and other ethnic and cultural groups, including gypsies and homosexuals, during the Holocaust. More recently, the term 'ethnic cleansing' has entered the lexicon as a description of what happened, for example, in the former Yugoslavia when ethnic nationalism replaced communism as the dominant force in the Balkans. This shift was epitomised in Bosnia, where Bosnian Serbs turned against Bosnian Muslims, systematically drove them from their homes and killed thousands in an attempt to assert the dominance of the Bosnian Serb ethnic group. National belonging and affiliation to Yugoslavia proved worthless in the face of ethnic nationalism.

The resurgence of ethnic nationalism over civic nationalism can also have an impact on the direction that theatre takes. Before independence in 1991, Tajikistan theatres served largely as hegemonic tools of the Soviet colonisers. Theatre functioned as part of civic nationalism to convey the interests of the state. In post-Soviet Tajikistan there has been a concerted campaign to revive a submerged ethnonational identity through a rejection of the previous state-imposed, Russian-influenced theatre in favour of a new, hybrid form of theatre deeply rooted in what is claimed to be an authentic Persian–Tajik tradition and its cultural heritage of music, dance and poetry. As this example demonstrates, the idea of a distinct national consciousness that persists through historical, political and social change is powerful, and this leads us to consider what we mean by the term 'national identity'.

National identity

In recent years, terms such as 'national character' and 'national consciousness' have been replaced by 'national identity', but the change in terminology does not make the phenomenon any easier to define. The ways in which individual members of a nation identify with their nation as national citizens relies on their engaging with national culture from a very early age. Echoing Gellner, Grosby explains,

> The child learns, for example, to speak the language of his or her nation and what it means to be a member of that nation as expressed through its customs and laws. These traditions become incorporated into the individual's understanding of the self. When those traditions that make up part of one's self-conception are shared by other individuals as part of their self-perception, one is then both related to those other individuals and aware of the relation. (*Nationalism*, p. 9)

Here, Grosby articulates a process that functions on a deep level of consciousness. In *Englishness and National Culture* (1999), Anthony Easthope likens it to being able to drive a car, when the mechanics of driving become curiously embodied and instinctual (pp. 3–4). In other words, we rarely think about our national identity, what it means and entails, but it is part and parcel of why we feel a sense of difference when we encounter other national cultures and of how we conduct ourselves on a daily basis. The topography of our towns and cities, whether we drive on the left- or right-hand side of the road, the food we eat, the currency we use and how we greet people are all tied up in our sense of national identity. In his 1995 book, Michael Billig refers to this as *Banal Nationalism*, habitually engrained in our social, political and cultural processes, which constitutes the unspoken, taken-for-granted national texture of our day-to-day encounters. But what about the feelings, the consciousness evoked by being a member of a nation, which can ignite fierce passions and loyalty?

The nation as imagined community

The German philosopher and literary critic Johann Gottfried von Herder was one of the first people to articulate the idea of a 'national soul'. This idea resurfaced in Ernest Renan's famous 1882 lecture 'What Is a Nation?', in which the French historian developed his idea of the nation as a 'spiritual principle' (Bhabha, *Nation and Narration*, p. 19). As Anwen Jones usefully highlights in *National Theatres in Context* (2007),

> The fact that Renan, one of the great heroes of the materialistic and mechanistic world of the nineteenth century, talks of the nation in such romantic and arguably religious or, at the very least, spiritual terms highlights both its magnetism and the difficulties inherent in articulating its allure in an objective fashion. (p. 3)

There is no denying that the very idea of the nation has a powerful emotional pull that is often difficult to articulate rationally. One of the most useful and ubiquitous theorists in this regard, Benedict Anderson, introduced the idea of the nation as an 'imagined community', which extends Renan's appeal to collectivity and an interconnected national moral conscience. The following passage captures the essence of Anderson's important idea. He argues that the nation is

> *imagined* because the members of even the smallest nation will never know most of their fellow-members, meet them or even hear of them, yet in the minds of each lives the image of their communion. ... It is imagined as a *community* because, regardless of the actual inequality and exploitation that may prevail in each, the nation is always conceived as a deep, horizontal comradeship.
> (*Imagined Communities*, 2nd edn, 2006, pp. 6–7)

Anderson's work provides a model for articulating how the huge scale of nations can have meaning for the individual at the level of imagining a massive form of common kinship. Yet there is a potential romanticism in Anderson's formulation, as it assumes that the imagination is inclusive and that people openly embrace other social identities based on differences of class, race and sexuality within the catchall of the nation – which is often very far from the case. It is also important to stress that the idea of the nation as imagined community should not deflect us from engaging with the nation as a political and social reality. At this stage, it is useful to recall Anderson's argument that the conjuring in the mind's eye of a deep horizontal citizenship explains people's willingness to kill and die for their nation in war. This point brings in the nation-state's role as political decision-maker (in the case of going to war) rather than reducing the nation to an abstract, amorphous mass. Other critics, notably Gopal Balakrishnan and Partha Chatterjee, have accused Anderson of undermining the stranglehold of the colonial imagination on how postcolonial nations are able to conceive of the nation. Nonetheless, Anderson's contribution to the field is extremely important because, as Jen Harvie writes in *Staging the UK* (2005), his particular mode of analysis

> locates the lived, social effects of national change not just in the major acts of nations' political institutions – the legislation of devolution and European unification, for example – but in the various cultural activities and structures people engage in, from reading newspapers, to shopping, to making or watching theatre performance. (p. 4)

National identity, then, is the meeting point between the individual and the collective conception of the nation, but crucially both are variable. An individual changes and alters his or her opinions, attitudes and levels of identification, and the nation is similarly an ongoing process.

The nation as ambivalent and hybrid identities

In *Nation and Narration*, Bhabha draws attention to the ambivalent nature of the nation. By this, he means that it is subject to competing discourses, change and periods of progress, regression and stasis. 'It is an ambivalence that emerges from a growing awareness that, despite the certainty with which historians speak of the "origins" of nation as a sign of the "modernity" of society, the cultural temporality of the nation inscribes a much more transitional social reality' (p. 1). The danger in summoning the nation as a known, unchanging entity is that it suggests harking back to some misplaced notion of national purity, when, in fact, the reality of the nation is reliant on its impurity, its ability to accommodate the mixing and blurring of cultures that make up the contemporary nation through migration, exile, transnationalism and globalisation. For Bhabha, this impurity leads to the presence of hybridised identities characterised by splitting, doubling and mixing. In our everyday lives, we see numerous examples of this, from the popularity of curry and chips to the dialects spoken by many young people in urban centres across Britain that merge the indigenous English language with Jamaican patois and Afro-Caribbean slang to create a new, rich, expressive language.

All this spotlights what the nation means for individuals in the contemporary world. On the one hand, people can embrace the changing character of the nation as a result of the movement of people. For instance, the choice of whether to eat at an Italian, Greek, Thai, French, Mexican, Japanese, Indian, Chinese or Malaysian restaurant that is open to most inhabitants of major cities throughout the world is a testament to such changes. However, such changes can also ignite feelings of alienation and fear and a nostalgic sense that the nation is not what it once was, and this can result in a retreat into xenophobic tribalism and a fear of other cultural groups that can spark violent national-ism. These issues are effectively explored in Roy Williams' plays, in particular *Sing Yer Heart Out for the Lads* (National Theatre, London, 2002), which addresses questions of race, belonging and national identity through the lens of a local pub football team and an England versus Germany football match. The play questions what it means to be English in the new millennium by acknowledging inner-city racial discord, casual racism and one character's bigoted opin-ion that '[i]f *they* want to practise *their* black culture and heritage, then they should be allowed to do it in *their* own part of *their* world' (Williams, *Sing Yer Heart Out for the Lads*, 2004, p. 188, my emphasis). But Williams pits this against the real complexities of interracial relationships, Black English patriotism and young Londoners picking and mixing eclectic cultural influences in the way they speak, the music they listen to and the personas they adopt. The reality is that *their* world is England and *their* black culture and heritage are part of and irrevocably changing English culture and heritage.

Similar theatrical treatments of the intersections between race and nationhood are available in Adrienne Kennedy's *Funnyhouse of a Negro* (East End Theater, New York, 1964), which tracks the central character, Sarah, as she negotiates

her identity as a young female of African American heritage in the United States during the 1960s. And forty years
later South African writer Beverley Naidoo produced *The
Playground* (Polka Theatre, London, 2004), which explores
the legacy of Apartheid. Developed in South Africa and fea-
turing a majority South African cast, the play tells the story
of Rosa, a ten-year-old girl whose mother sends her to be
one of the first black children at an all-white school following Nelson Mandela's integration laws of the mid-1990s. It
offers a moving account of racial identification, discrimination and acceptance in a rapidly evolving national context.

The national, the local and the global

Stuart Hall, among others, draws attention to the competing
pressures that the forces of globalisation exert on the nation.
He highlights the tensions between capitalism's transnational
imperatives and its powerful residual promotion of awareness of the nation-state and national cultures. This duality
has been a concern for workers across the world, particularly during the recent global economic crisis, as they have
been understandably far more sensitive to the effects of the
international labour market on national job prospects. As
politics and economics become ever more global, the appeal
of the local expands exponentially. Opposition to the effects
of market-led globalisation – whether environmental or in
terms of the local street scene – are manifest in smaller,
quieter acts such as attending farmers markets and tend-
ing allotments, which undermine the brash, high-profile
commercialism of McDonald's and Wal-Mart, which has

'8000 retail units under 55 different banners in 15 countries' (www.walmartstores.com).

The community-led Transition Town movement, which strives in its everyday action to address climate change by promoting ways to move from a high-carbon to a low-carbon economy through local food production and sustainable living, is a good example of the forward march of the local (www.transitionculture.org). Rob Hopkins, who developed the idea in 2003, established the first Transition Town in Totnes in Devon, England, in 2006. Totnes also became the first town to launch its own currency, accepted only by local businesses, to support the local economy. If this rings the alarm bells of parochial insularity Dan Rebellato warns against in *Theatre & Globalization* (2009), it is important to stress that the movement engages with the particularities of local communities but has a global reach. Transition Town has become an international phenomenon and facilitated a globally significant network, with the 100th franchise being established in Fujino, Japan, and other transition towns emerging in Canada, the United States and Italy. If nothing else, the Transition Town movement highlights the responsiveness of people, local communities and international networks to changing global, economic and environmental circumstances. If the nation, as Stuart Hall argues in 'Whose Heritage?' (2005), 'is an ongoing project, under constant revision' (p. 24), then adaptation is essential. Hall suggests that a nation has 'finite, if elastic borders', and this sense of an 'elastic nation' offers a useful way of thinking about how the nation stretches to incorporate new social movements, new ethnicities, political changes and the emergence of cultures of hybridity that enrich and irreversibly alter 'indigenous' national cultures.

Let us now turn our attention to the ways that this theoretical terrain has found a platform in theatre.

National theatres and state-of-the-nation plays

In an attempt to summarise the key characteristics of nationalism, Smith argues that the following meanings of the term took root during the twentieth century:

(1) a process of formation, or growth, of nations;
(2) a sentiment or consciousness of belonging to the nation;
(3) a language and symbolism of the nation;
(4) a social and political movement on behalf of the nation;
(5) a doctrine and/or ideology of the nation, both general and particular. (*Nationalism*, p. 5)

The characteristics Smith identifies are closely connected. The first refers to the creation of the nation that forms the object of the other four categories. The second refers to the feelings evoked by being a member of a nation and to the sense of belonging and identity this brings. The language and symbolism of the nation are the dominant discourses surrounding that nation and the markers that distinguish nations, such as flags, anthems, national dress and currency, as well as national landmarks, monuments and buildings. As a social and political movement, nationalism is an awareness of and support for the particular culture of a nation through organisations and activities that promote national histories, language and arts and can be part of a wider political nationalist campaign for greater independence or power on the global stage. All these characteristics relate to the ideology of nationalism, which 'serves to give force and direction to both symbols and movements' (p. 8) by emphasising the centrality of the nation as a mode of thinking and action that stresses the importance of national autonomy and national identity. All these meanings have surfaced in the way that the national theatre movement has evolved.

The common conception of a national theatre is of a high-profile building in a capital city brimming with civic pride and cultural prominence, producing works by national playwrights and theatre-makers in shows that exude high production values because of their sizable government subsidies. Yet writers such as Marvin Carlson, Bruce McConachie and Steve Wilmer make it clear that the history of national theatres is multiple, as 'each National Theatre was unique in that it reflected a specific originating moment, location, set of goals, language, history, and mythology, as well as the idiosyncratic beliefs of its individual founding members' (Wilmer, *National Theatres in a Changing Europe*, 2008, p. 9). National theatres are also subject to shifting historical circumstances in terms of the rise and fall of nation-states, redrawn national borders and ideological battles.

The origins of national theatres, as we understand them today, are in the court theatres of the seventeenth and eighteenth centuries, when the material theatrical culture of the nation reflected the interests of those in power. There was little room for democratic principles in these buildings, let alone dissent. The Comédie-Française, founded by Louis XIV in 1680 in Paris to perform works by the major French dramatists Molière, Racine and Corneille, is, according to Bruce McConachie in his 2008 essay 'Towards a History of National Theatres in Europe', generally regarded as the 'granddaddy of European monarchical theatres' (p. 52). It set the scene for a number of royal institutions designed to 'entertain the elite with plays, operas, and ballets that reflected their aristocratic values' (Wilmer, *National Theatres in a Changing Europe*, p. 1). In Austria, the Burgtheater, founded by Empress Maria Theresa in 1741, sat adjacent to the imperial palace, underlining its prestige and importance for sustaining imperial power and the status quo. The Royal Theatre in Copenhagen, which opened in 1748, followed these autocratic, elite value systems, although it broke the mould when it began to commission and promote work by Danish playwrights rather than the more usual Italian and French playwrights and theatre troupes.

After admiring the indigenous repertoire of the Royal Theatre in Copenhagen, the German writer Johann Elias Schlegel touted it as a potential model for an emergent German national theatre that could reach a broad German populace. In 1767, the foundation of the Hamburg National Theatre heralded a new form of municipal theatre that extended its reach to the bourgeoisie as a way of disseminating national values and culture. Although short lived, this theatre showed how a theatre could dedicate itself to producing work that represented a unique national character through its focus on German national history, characters, language and repertoire. This conception of a uniquely German style of theatre is fascinating, and it raises questions about what makes a theatre, play or performance 'national'. These questions certainly circulated around the Mannheim National Theatre (1779), where the young dramatist Friedrich Schiller worked.

The intellectual roots of nationalism and its manifestation in national theatres are in eighteenth-century Romantic theory, particularly that propounded by Rousseau in France and Schiller in Germany. Indeed, the idea that theatre could not only represent the nation but be a vital tool of nation-building found a high-profile and tireless campaigner in Schiller, who proposed,

> If in all our plays there was one main stream,
> if our poets reached an agreement and created
> a firm union for this final purpose – if a strict
> selection led their work and their brushes dedic-
> ated themselves only to national matters – in one
> word, if we had a national stage, we would also
> become a nation. (Quoted in Wilmer, *National
> Theatres in a Changing Europe*, p. 15)

In her 2008 essay 'The National Stage and the Naturalized House' Loren Kruger highlights problems with this position. As she writes, 'Schiller's declaration rests on the assumption that the nation-to-be-created is already present, singular, and distinct in the minds of those creating it, even though its actual absence from their lives suggest that its distinctive character is as yet imagined – or invented' (p. 37). Nonetheless, the French and American revolutions instigated nationalist movements throughout the world as nations were encouraged to see the goal of increased autonomy and self-determination as achievable. For many countries, the theatre became a site for exploring and representing a burgeoning cultural nationalism and a means of contributing to and legitimising broader political campaigns. Drawing on the work of Johann Gottfried von Herder, who encouraged cultural thinkers, producers and artists to seek out that which could mark out their nation as unique and distinctive, many cultural workers put their efforts behind campaigns to remember and retrieve their national cultural heritage through submerged folk traditions, folklore, myths and legends. As Eric Hobsbawm remarks in his introduction to *The Invention of Tradition* (1983), these folk traditions 'were modified, ritualized and institutionalized for the new national purposes' (p. 6). This impulse to look backwards served many aims: it claimed cultural distinctiveness, fostered a sense of pride in cultural traditions and authenticated national identity by furnishing it with longevity. However, the cultural foundations on which this ideal has been built are shaky to say the least.

Cultural nationalism: the *Poems of Ossian* and beyond

Ernest Renan knew that '[t]o forget and – I will venture to say – to get one's history wrong, are essential factors in the making of a nation' (quoted in Wilmer, *Writing and Rewriting National Theatre Histories*, 2004, p. ix). In Scotland, James Macpherson achieved notoriety through his 'discovery' of the epic *Poems of Ossian* in the 1760s, which he had, in fact, largely written himself. Despite being one of history's greatest literary hoaxes, Macpherson's fraudulent attempt to construct a literary heritage for the Highlands as a counter-discourse to the narratives of loss and degradation following the brutal Clearances and the suppression of Gaelic identity had a transnational impact by influencing writers, composers, artists and the development of the Romantic movement. Macpherson did excavate and make known existing manuscripts and a rich Gaelic oral tradition of folklore and ballads, but he also exploited a latent desire for a literary work to rival Homer's *Iliad* and *Odyssey* by fabricating an epic poem of war, heroism, defeat and resilience. Based on Gaelic tradition and Celtic mythology, the Ossianic works tapped into a market for a 'genuine', cohesive cultural rehabilitation for the Highlands; more importantly, the poems proved malleable in different cultural contexts, as their extensive local, national and global success and reverberations prove. As Robert Crawford insists,

> The whole argument about Ossian being a hoax I just find utterly boring. The more we view Ossian as made-up, the more impressive the achievement becomes in terms of imaginative literature. The European, the North American, the Indian impact of the Ossianic works is absolutely

> remarkable. No sane person would now regard
> the Ossianic poems as accurate historical docu-
> ments, they are works of imagination and, as
> such, they have been remarkably powerful.
> (*Ossian*, BBC Radio 4, broadcast 3 May 2009)

The international reach of the Ossian poems is worth dwelling on for a little longer as it raises some interesting issues. As I have already indicated, the danger with cultural projects that claim to retrieve a lost national cultural con-sciousness is that they rely on essentialist and exclusion-ary notions of identity, as if countries remain hermetically sealed from outside influences in a mythical continuation of cultural, linguistic and national purity. At its most extreme, this can mean excluding and suppressing elements and people within a culture, as with the persecution of the Jewish population and their culture during the German Nazi regime, or it can result in a simple failure to acknowledge the transnational cross-fertilisation of ideas and practices. Loren Kruger argues that national theatres have 'always existed in a *transnational* field' ('The National Stage and the Naturalized House', p. 35). Whether we are talking about debates around the authority of cultural products providing models of cultural practice for other countries or concerns over tourists rather than national citizens being the primary recipients of the national theatre product, transnational agendas inform the theory and practice of national theatres. From the early model of the Comédie-Française to the dis-semination of Schiller's arguments for a national theatre to the national theatres emerging in the postcolonial moment, each has drawn inspiration from transnational perspectives in terms of location, repertoire and audience (p. 35).

Macpherson's model, if not his methods, persisted and had a marked impact on theatre as many dramatists turned to submerged cultural traditions and folk culture for their inspiration. For instance, Elias Lönnrut collected folk songs and reconfigured them into the *Kalevala*, a Homeresque narrative. And at the Abbey Theatre in Dublin, which opened in 1904, W. B. Yeats and Lady Gregory dedicated themselves to disseminating Celtic mythology, folklore and legend, and to romanticising rural life in the West of Ireland as a way of asserting a distinct cultural, linguistic and political identity as part of a wider campaign for autonomy from a dominant foreign culture.

Political turbulence characterised the early years of the twentieth century and temporarily disbanded the national theatre project, only for it to re-emerge with a vengeance in the middle of the century in association with newly acquired political independence in African and Asia. The Korean National Theatre opened in 1950, two years after independence. Nasser created the National Theatre of Egypt in 1953 after an upsurge in nationalist sentiment following the end of direct British colonial rule. In Senegal, Léopold Senghor established a national theatre in Dakar fives years after the country achieved independence from France in 1960. However, as Marvin Carlson argues in his 2008 essay 'National Theatres: Then and Now', the legacy of colonialism and issues of ownership and repertoire persisted; many of these theatres were compromised by their adherence to Western, largely European, models as a way of asserting their European-inspired cultural values (p. 27). A similar argument informs Sudipto Chatterjee's discussion in 'The Nation Staged' (2009) of Bengali theatre from the late nineteenth century that sought to mimic colonial English theatres. Thus, according to Carlson and Chatterjee, these theatres were less indigenous expressions of cultural independence and national pride than the bearers of markers of subordination and an internalised sense of cultural inferiority – an observation that recalls Partha Chatterjee's criticism of Benedict Anderson in the 1996 essay 'Whose Imagined Community?', which foregrounds questions about who has the power to imagine and who sets the terms of this imaginative terrain.

The drive to conceive new models of the national theatre has been the rationale for many of the national theatres that emerged during the latter half of the twentieth century and into the twenty-first century – the subject of the following section.

National theatres and democratisation

A primary challenge to the conception of the national theatre emerged during the twentieth century and has continued into the twenty-first century: the question of whether a single theatre, normally in a national capital, can legitimately claim to serve as a theatre of and for the nation as a whole. In Anderson's terms, is it possible to conceive of a theatre that can sufficiently imagine the nation in and through its repertoire? In *The National Stage* (1992), Kruger draws attention to the frankly rather dubious assumption that a national theatre audience can legitimately represent the nation as a synecdoche of national citizenship. As she writes, 'The idea of representing the nation in theatre, of summoning a representative audience that will in turn recognize itself as nation on stage, offers a compelling if ambiguous image of national unity, less as an indisputable fact than as an object of speculation' (p. 3). It is fair to say that a typical national theatre audience will undoubtedly have multifaceted identities; it will probably include people who identify themselves as national citizens as well as some for whom the term is ambiguous at best – not to mention a high proportion of international tourists, whose national affiliations, if any, reside elsewhere. Are national theatres representative of the wider populace in terms of the key identifiers of age, race, regionality and class? If they are not, can we regard them as national theatres? And what about the material that appears on the stages of national theatres? What and whom does a national theatre represent? Whose stories are told, and why are these the stories that a nation needs to narrate? How many national citizens can a national theatre credibly claim to reach given its location, repertoire and cost?

These concerns have led to a growing decentralising and democratising impulse. During the mid-twentieth century, a series of state-supported theatres emerged throughout France as part of André Malraux' plan to decentralise the arts to the outskirts of Paris, its suburbs and other cities. When the director Jean Vilar resigned from the Paris-based

Théâtre National Populaire, the government initially tried to persuade Roger Planchon to uproot from Villeurbanne, a suburb of Lyon where he founded the Théâtre de la Cité, a 'people's theatre' designed to bring culture to as wide a spectrum of people as possible. After Planchon refused to leave his home town to take over, the government simply transferred the prestigious and generously funded Théâtre National Populaire to Villeurbanne in 1972 – a prime example of decentralisation in practice.

One of the first devolved models appeared in Australia in 1968, when the government decided to support not a single national theatre but an umbrella organisation that would facilitate and nurture theatre across the country rather than in the metropolitan centre. Similarly, Finland established eight regional theatres in 1978, which had touring as part of their remit. There was no longer an expectation that people would go to their national theatre; the national theatre network should go to the people. More recently, the National Theatre of Scotland, launched in 2006 following the momentous advent of devolution in 1999, has approached decentralisation in an innovative fashion. With no dedicated building, the National Theatre of Scotland remains a fleet-footed organisation that collaborates with the existing theatrical infrastructure of Scotland to produce small- and large-scale text-based theatre, community-based theatre, children's theatre, site-responsive theatre, multigenerational, multi-focused and, importantly, multi-sited work that is free to roam the nation and overseas.

The National Theatre of Scotland's ethos of inclusion means that it supports works such as the internationally acclaimed *Black Watch* (University of Edinburgh Drill Hall, 2006) by Gregory Burke, which moves between Fife and Fallujah in its theatrically dynamic exploration of the cultural heritage at the heart of the Black Watch regiment and the harsh realities of life on the front line. It also supported the recent *Transform* series, which built on the inaugural production, *Home* (2006), which consisted of ten productions in ten locations in Scotland, involving ten collaborations with other artists and companies. One hundred and fifty high school students and local people created *Transform Caithness*, a site-responsive journey around Thurso, and Dennis Kelly's *Our Teacher's a Troll* (Mull Theatre, Druimfin, 2009) toured to the over-fives in small theatres and village halls. At the National Theatre of Scotland, national citizens, playwrights, artists, theatre-makers and creative producers collaborate to put on a rich programme of events that encapsulate the multiple communities that constitute the Scottish nation in a way that is outward looking, forward thinking and internationally significant.

The National Theatre of Wales, launched in November 2009, has similarly adopted a building-less model. It plans, from its opening show, *A Good Night Out in the Valleys* (Bedwas Workman's Hall, Caerphilly, 2010), to take diverse theatre practices to alternative sites across the country, such as a beach in north Wales and a military range in the Brecon Beacons, to 'theatrically map Wales' (www.nationaltheatrewales.org). Both theatres recognise that nations are complex heterogeneous entities with many geographical communities, interest groups and theatrical traditions.

National theatres for changing times

National theatres have faced enormous challenges as they respond to and accommodate changing social, cultural and economic conditions. Globalisation, migration, devolution, multiculturalism, identity politics, multilingualism and new technologies have had a profound impact on the meaning of the nation, leading Dragan Klaic to argue in 'National Theatres Undermined by the Withering of the Nation-State' (2008) that 'the term National Theatre has become a rather arbitrary, almost meaningless label, an anachronistic, exhausted ideological construct' (p. 220). Indeed, the whole idea of the national theatre, as the national theatres of Scotland and Wales testify, has been remodelled and encapsulates Janelle Reinelt's stress in 'The Role of National Theatres in the Age of Globalization' (2008) on 'a network of theatrical sites' engaged in the production, play and performance of national identities (p. 229). Yet it is interesting to note that in a global context in which it is increasingly difficult to say what the term 'nation' stands for, rather than being 'exhausted', as Klaic argues, the term 'national theatre' is still fought for as a way of signalling cultural autonomy, distinctiveness and legitimacy, particularly where, as in Scotland and Wales, national cultures have felt subsumed by a dominant neighbour. As Dai Smith, chairman of Arts Council Wales, commented regarding the Welsh National Theatre, 'We have been putting our toes in the water for too long. It was inexcusable, outrageous, that we did not have a national theatre for Wales. It may be 100 years late, but better late than not at all' (quoted in Mark Brown, 'Wales Raises Curtain on £3m National Theatre,' *Guardian* 5 November 2009, p. 6).

The other principal concept that concretely binds theatre and nation together is the state-of-the-nation play or production, which is the focus of the next section.

State-of-the-nation plays

In his 2008 essay 'From the State of the Nation to Globalization', Dan Rebellato draws attention to the fact that there is 'no established formal definition of the state-of-the-nation play' (p. 246); it is one of those things that we know when we see it. Alongside the large casts, public settings, epic timescales and national venues that Rebellato identifies with the state-of-the-nation play, critics primarily apply the term to works that have the nation, preferably in some sort of rupture, crisis or conflict, at their core. In general terms, the state-of-the-nation play deploys representations of personal events, family structures and social or political organisations as a microcosm of the nation-state to comment directly or indirectly on the ills befalling society, on key narratives of nationhood or on the state of the nation as it wrestles with changing circumstances.

State-of-the-nation plays take many forms internationally, from psychologically rich social realism, through magic realism, to multimedia productions that fuse live and recorded action. In the United States, key examples are Arthur Miller's *Death of a Salesman* (Morosco Theatre, New York, 1949), an acute dissection of America and the American Dream through the microcosm of the Loman family, and Tony Kushner's *Angels in America: A Gay Fantasia on National Themes* (Eureka Theatre, San Francisco, 1991). The latter, an epic, sprawling play, merges domestic narratives with a fantasy world of visiting angels, ghosts and hallucinations to tackle issues of sexuality, race, class and religion in the shadow of the aggressive free-market Republicanism that marked American politics in the 1980s. In South Africa we might think of Athol Fugard's stripped bare *Sizwe Bansi Is Dead* (The Space, Cape Town, 1972), written in collaboration with two African actors, John Kani and Winston Ntshona (both of whom appeared in the original production), which is a scathing attack on the treatment of the black community during the Apartheid era, and of Jane Taylor's theatrically extravagant *Ubu and the Truth Commission* (Market Theatre, Johannesburg, 1997), created with the director William Kentridge and the Handspring Puppet Company, which deployed live action, music, animation and documentary materials to satirise the origins, ethics and potential consequences of South Africa's Truth and Reconciliation Commission for individuals and the national psyche.

For many theatre critics and commentators, the state-of-the-nation play is the most valid form of theatrical output. For instance, in *State of the Nation: British Theatre since 1945* (2007), the British theatre critic Michael Billington makes a strong case for work that explicitly debates the interplay of theatre and society, where theatre can hold a mirror up to nation, find it wanting and offer a robust, preferably unfunny, preferably social-realist, critique of its failings. In his account, Billington favours an emphasis on upheaval and turbulence in chapters entitled 'Theatre of Opposition', 'Winters of Discontent' and 'Scenes from an Execution'. It is as though the nation, and its representation in theatre, is an interesting object of study only when there is trouble afoot.

Like many, Billington believes passionately in the potential of theatre not only to reflect society but also to provoke social transformation by shedding light on issues of morality and ethics. This is a view developed by Jill Dolan in *Utopia in Performance* (2005). Yet Dolan moves away from Billington's obsession with thesis, argument and pronouncement to explore what live theatre feels like – how it evokes pleasure, exhilaration and a sense of connection with others. For Dolan theatre is a place where people might 'share experiences of meaning making and imagination that can describe or capture fleeting intimations of a better world' (p. 2). Dolan argues that theatre and performance have the capacity to move beyond the national paradigm that Billington clings on to, to inspire audience members to feel 'allied with each other, and with a broader, more capacious sense of a public' that can promote 'a more abstracted notion of "community," or ... an even more intangible idea of "humankind"' (p. 2). Dolan's approach harnesses the power of theatre as an imaginative, creative, communal, expansive, ephemeral and ever-evolving process.

The following section connects Billington's emphasis on theatre, society and turbulence with Dolan's emphasis on theatrical affect by addressing a core strand of state-of-the-nation productions: those that take riots and their aftermath as a starting-point.

Nations under duress

This section starts from the premise that the nation comes under particular scrutiny during moments of social break-down and urban unrest that unsettle any idea of the homogeneous nation by revealing the fractures caused by racial discord, socioeconomic differences and abuse of power. Riots are intriguing social phenomena that emerge at times of acute sociopolitical tension to cause often extensive personal, social and material damage. Highly theatrical in nature, these communal outbursts of public disorder are all about enactment, display and commanding an audience for the dissent they embody.

During and immediately after a riot, or series of riots, there is an overwhelming sense that a nation must be sick in some way for these festering sores to erupt throughout the body of the nation. In assessing the source of riots, social commentators highlight contributory factors that expose the fragility of the nation and the myth of a cohesive national symbolic community unified by a common goal and purpose. Riots instigate moments of national crisis; however, as Reinelt writes in 'Notes for a Radical Democratic Theater' (1998), 'crisis' can be 'an enabling state of acute tension, opening a space of indeterminacy in conceptions, institutions, and practices formerly regarded as viable or at least entrenched. Crisis threatens to destabilize these social structures, often leading to the experience of anomie and disintegration, but also to a creative uncertainty' (p. 284). Interestingly, Renan also argued in 'What Is a Nation?' for the importance of crisis in establishing and maintaining the nation: 'where national memories are concerned, griefs are of more value than triumphs' (p. 19). In the case of riots, the nation is thrown into disarray, but in the aftermath of these uncertain times modes of looking and being can be recast as the nation seeks to reassert itself in the contemporary moment.

What purpose can theatre serve in this aftermath? How can theatre usefully engage in the reappraisal and restaging of the nation? On one level, as the newspaper articles fade from view, theatre, in its temporal distance from the moment of unrest, can act as a form of cultural witnessing, as an acknowledgement and a reminder that this national event happened at all, that there was enough strength of feeling for people to occupy public spaces, burn cars, throw stones and deface buildings. Physically rather than verbally articulate, riots function on the visceral level of the scream: they are highly expressive, but time is required to find the source and the meaning of the expression, to uncover its intricacies. Theatre offers a site where creative practitioners can explore, assess and interrogate the genesis, complexities and ramifications of these inarticulate expressions, a space to find another form of articulacy that can speak of and to these moments of crisis.

From small-scale community theatre projects to the blockbuster megamusical *Les Misérables*, riotous outbreaks have provided a fertile vein of source material for theatre practitioners to explore community breakdown as a way of commenting more broadly on a nation's political agenda, trajectory, socioeconomic inequalities, cultural history or race relations. This section centres on case studies of Mohamed Rouabhi's *Vive la France!* (Théâtre Gerard Philipe, Saint-Denis, 2005) and Anna Deavere Smith's *Fires in the Mirror: Crown Heights, Brooklyn and Other Identities* (Joseph Papp Public Theatre, New York, 1992), but first I want to consider a wider body of state-of-the-nation plays that employ riots as source material.

Max Sparber's *Minstrel Show; Or, The Lynching of William Brown* (Douglas County Courthouse, Omaha, 1998) takes the Omaha race riot of 1919 as its source. Premiered in the Douglas County Courthouse, the site of the flare-up of racial tension that culminated in the brutal lynching of African American William Brown, who stood accused of raping a young white woman, the play subsequently toured throughout America. In the play, events are re-told through the eyes and distinctive vocal characters of two fictional African American variety entertainers. The play received a controversial reception for the way it embraced black minstrelsy as a valuable cultural form, but it succeeded in reclaiming an important moment in local and national African American history, while also considering the racial and cultural politics of minstrelsy as a performance mode in the wider context of a troubled race relations history.

A verbatim theatre piece based on extensive research in Burnley in the north of England to uncover the legacy of the riots that erupted there in 2001, *Mixed Up North* by Robin Soans (MacOwan Theatre, London, 2008) has toured England extensively following its origins as an Out of Joint/London Academy of Music and Dramatic Arts collaboration. *Mixed Up North* uses a familiar play-within-a-play structure in which a Burnley-based multiracial youth group plan to stage a show about mixed-race relationships, but it subverts this modus operandi when the show is aborted at the dress rehearsal and a public question-and-answer session is held in its place. Highlighting issues of economic deprivation, disaffected youth, the grooming of young white girls by older Asian men and racial discord, this meta-theatrical work considers the potential efficacy of cultural initiatives that play the long game in tackling racial discord rather than looking for quick fixes or sensational media headlines.

Performed during a period of acute political scrutiny into the success or otherwise of Britain's multicultural project, *Mixed Up North* provides a space for the people directly affected by the Burnley riots to speak out. In this sense, they occupy a public, albeit theatrical, platform normally given over to voices of authority that attempt to appraise and summarise the issues in a way that is rarely nuanced by the reality of lived experience in areas of acute social disturbance. A similar impetus drove Karen Therese's *The Riot Act* (Campbelltown Arts Centre, New South Wales, 2009), which employs verbatim theatre techniques, alongside multimedia and physical theatre, to tackle personal, institutional and media responses to three highly publicised riots that took place across New South Wales in Bidwill, Redfern and Macquarie Fields. Building on a series of creative development residencies that enabled Therese to solicit opinions from residents, youth workers, social workers, police and media workers, *The Riot Act* poetically intervenes in the social and media-based narratives that emerged to explain the riots and their consequences for the local communities.

Immigration and eruption: Mohamed Rouabhi's *Vive la France!*

In 2005 the death by electrocution of two teenagers, Zyed Benna and Bouna Traoré, who climbed into an electrical sub-station in an attempt to hide from police, prompted riots in the Paris suburb of Clichy-sous-Bois, which is densely populated with African and Arab communities. After police launched a tear-gas grenade which hit a mosque, anger spread and unrest crept across the Seine-Saint-Denis region into three other parts of Paris before spreading beyond Paris to the eastern city of Dijon and other areas in southern and western France. The riots reached such a scale that on 8 November 2005 President Jacques Chirac announced a national state of emergency. Poverty, unemployment, racial discrimination, immigration and heavy-handed policing all contributed to the climate of unrest. Azouz Begag, minister for the promotion of equal opportunity, accused Nicolas Sarkozy, then the interior minister, of 'warlike semantics' after he announced a 'zero tolerance' policy towards the 'scum' perpetrating civil unrest. This public disagreement signalled the extent to which France was in a state of internal national rupture, unable to cope with the competing discourses around its national politics and identity.

These riots demonstrated the alienation felt by many immigrant communities living in France. Rather than Hall's model of the elastic nation, whereby nations grow and morph to accommodate new ethnicities, France was accused of fostering either 'exclusionary or assimilationist conceptions of immigrant integration' (Will Kymlicka, 'Liberal Nationalism and Cosmopolitan Justice', 2008, p. 136). Certainly, the riots followed a series of controversies over the French government's failure to embrace an inclusive notion of national citizenship that could accommodate immigrant ethnicity in schools and the workplace in the form of dress codes, public holidays and multicultural educational practices. In these controversies, Seyla Benhabib, in *Another Cosmopolitanism* (2008), detected a shift away from the forms of multicultural nationhood that theorists such as Bhabha, Hall and Gilroy argue are an integral component of the contemporary landscape.

In the immediate aftermath of the riots, the political playwright and theatre-maker Mohamed Rouabhi began work on *Vive la France!* Co-produced by the Cité Nationale de l'Histoire de l'Immigration, staged six months after the riots and dedicated to Benna and Traoré, the piece offered a coruscating assault on the politics of immigration, the legacy of colonialism and the failure of France to extend its commitment to the Universal Declaration of Human

Rights to all its national citizens. The title, which translates as 'Long Live France', ironically draws on the revolutionary calls for a France of liberty, equality and fraternity, but *Vive la France!*'s content exposes the maintenance of inequalities within the republic. 'According to Rouabhi, the most destructive result of such inequalities is scorn, the kind that leaves its victims speechless, consequently unable to respond to their adversaries in an attempt to break down the barriers that divide' (Molly Grogan, 'Theater Director Mohamed Rouabhi's France'). In *Vive la France!* Rouabhi gives voice and representation to the marginalised immigrant communities of France and explores the roots that cause and the social practices that perpetuate their unstable place within the nation-state.

Rouabhi's contestatory, critical and provocative work is fragmentary, elusive and partial. He relies on a collage of appropriated material, including images, songs, political speeches, clandestine video footage, critical theory, poetry, rap and extracts from film and television, interspersed with scenes driven by his creative writing. Criss-crossing different historical moments, cultural signifiers, critical thinkers, and high and popular culture, Rouabhi's aesthetic is about making connections across the fragments, having one image or piece of text illuminate another through placement and juxtaposition. As one spectator explained, 'The experience was more like hopping between channels but where each scene imprints its dazzling image on your retina, even if just in a flash, and where each new image engraves itself over the last to create dense layers or meaning, interconnection, a feeling of total sensory overload' (Mary Stevens, http://marysresearchblog.wordpress.com/2006/12/04/vive-la-france-by-mohammed-rouabhi/).

One scene of *Vive la France!*, based on a reading of Frantz Fanon's explosive *Black Skin, White Masks*, first published in 1952, offers an analysis of the impact of colonialism on black subjectivity, intercut with extracts from television interviews with Harry Roselmack, the first black man to host French primetime news. In another sequence, a middle-aged black woman positions herself centre-stage and removes her dressing gown to reveal her naked form. In this revelatory moment the audience is challenged to take in her body – her form, her colour, her femininity, her humanity. In this simple act Rouabhi challenges his French audience to confront the presence of the black body in its midst, to recognise its familiarity, its fleshly appearance. There is also footage from an amateur video recording of the brutal beating of a young man by French security forces during the 2005 riots. This material is ironically followed by a pop tribute to France's police recorded by Annie Cordy in 1977, 'Mon C.R.S'.

In another scene, video footage from 1974 shows a young, white, male hippy with long hair walking through the countryside admiring the natural world and expressing the need to find the common humanity in all people. In the immediate context, the inclusion of this piece suggests a bitter critique of lost idealism and an admonishment of a nation that has politically repositioned itself to the right and strengthened the literal and cultural borders that divide people. Explicitly connecting the re-emergence of xenophobic nationalism with Vichy's National Revolution and highlighting the ideological affinities between Sarkozy and French National Front politicians Jean-Marie Le Pen and his daughter Marine Le Pen, Rouabhi invites his audience to question the values that have shaped France in the past and continue to shape France in the twenty-first century. As Grogan writes, *Vive la France!* 'functions as both a trip back in time to the vast reaches of French colonial empire and a careful reflection on the prejudices, fears and stereotypes which narrowly define the space and identities conferred, in reality, by the French Republic to its citizens of color' ('Theater Director Mohamed Rouabhi's France'). Above all, Rouabhi's intervention is one means of refusing to brush under the carpet the events that started in Clichy-sous-Bois but had reverberations throughout France. Rather than retreating into a collective silence and quickly reassembling the veneer of national unity, Rouabhi picks at the wound, tears off the scab and demands a national dialogue that confronts the nation's most awkward truths. A similar refusal to ignore tensions in the national psyche regarding race and multicultural communities informs Smith's *Fires in the Mirror: Crown Heights, Brooklyn and Other Identities*, discussed next.

Searching for the American character: Anna Deavere Smith's *Fires in the Mirror*

At the forefront of theatre seeking literally to give voice to the dynamics of conflict and the dysfunctional dimensions of the nation sits the African American theatre-maker Anna Deavere Smith. Smith's work, for which she has adopted the collective title *On the Road: A Search for American Character*, offers a provocative assault on America's struggle to address the multifarious issues of gender, race, sexuality and class unsettling and destabilising its communities. Importantly, her work highlights not only differences and the social cleavages these differences open up but also how people negotiate difference in often difficult and fraught circumstances. On a community level, Smith's work is often brutally revealing of the fissures and volatility beneath the surface of organisations and geographical areas. Smith's theatrical processes have legitimised her voice as an African American women engaged in a critical commentary on American values and the pursuit of democratic citizenship, to the extent that Reinelt argues that she has been constructed by the media as an authority on the 'tensions in American life' ('Notes for a Radical Democratic Theater', p. 291).

After starting her *On the Road* series in 1982, Smith developed her reputation by creating work in response to specific events or commissions that required her to investigate geographical, work-based or identificatory communities. Smith draws her material from extensive interviews with people directly or indirectly connected to an event, area or institution, and her aesthetic relies on her ability to research, collate, edit and theatrically interpret a diverse range of voices. The intricacies and individuality of the voice are incredibly important for Smith. In performance, she engages in a scrupulous re-pronouncement of the rhythmic speech patterns and verbal idiosyncrasies of the people she interviews, anxious to represent her version of them as they appeared to her. Acquired through a process of insistent reiteration, Smith's ability to capture the nuances – and often eloquent inarticulacy – of individual speech works to assert the presence of various identities; it also offers an interesting take on the position of the subject as she morphs across age, gender, race and class, performatively playing with the mutability of identity (Carol Martin, 'Bearing Witness', 1996, p. 82). The polyphonic quality of her work also captures the complexity of community formation as Smith's work reminds the spectator that the different people she embodies all occupy the same space/community – they are, in effect, all America.

Smith's readiness to adopt multiple subject positions is suggestive of a liberalism – an openness to different viewpoints. It is as if she puts everything on the table and then turns to her audience to say, 'Okay, so where from here?' These differences of perspective are not reconcilable, resolvable; there is no potential consensus. But for the nation to function, a way has to be found through the coexistence of multiple subject positions. Above all, Smith is a provocateur who shows the 'critical dissensus' – to adopt Chantal Mouffe's term from *Dimensions of Radical Democracy* (1992) – in the communities she stages, with a view to stimulating debate and tentative negotiation rather than simple solutions to local or national dilemmas. Mouffe argues for the necessity of antagonism as a marker of true democratic process, and in her work Smith reiterates the creative potential of using conflictual situations as a way of making difference known and better understood.

In an interview with Carol Martin, Smith addressed the difficult social consequences of racial difference in America, arguing that 'there are too many contradictions, problems, and lies in American society about the melting pot' ('Bearing Witness', p. 194). Such tensions ignited a violent outburst in the Crown Heights area of Brooklyn in August 1991 after a Hasidic man lost control of his car and mounted the pavement, killing Gavin Cato, a seven-year-old black child. Shortly afterwards, Yankel Rosenbaum, a Hasidic rabbinical student, was stabbed and killed by a member of the black community in an act of retaliation. 'The ensuing riots that wracked Crown Heights' previous atmosphere of tolerance for its divergent cultures made national headlines and pointed to the growing friction in racial and cultural relations across America' (*Fires in the Mirror*, back cover). Commissioned by the Public Theatre in New York, Smith almost immediately set to work creating *Fires in the Mirror: Crown Heights, Brooklyn and Other Identities* to contribute to a period of national self-reflection and reappraisal.

Smith based *Fires in the Mirror* on interviews with a range of people including creative artists, professors, church ministers, activists, community workers and members of the Crown Heights community. With an overhead display providing the names of the people played by Smith, the first section captures people as they ruminate on identity, belonging, cultural representation, the legacy of slavery, religious persecution and community. The second section of the work, devoted to the events in Crown Heights, provides a multi-perspectival account of the causes and aftermath of the riots that wracked Crown Heights, with individuals from both sides in the dispute venting their sense of racial discrimination and discord in extremely powerful and emotive ways through Smith's mediation. In one sequence, Smith plays Yankel Rosenbaum's brother at a rally in New York, where his words imply that the American nation is as much a victim as his brother:

> When my brother was surrounded,
> Each and every American was surrounded.
> When my brother was stabbed four times,
> Each and every American was stabbed four times. (p. 103)

Collapsing the boundaries between the individual and the nation, this small moment underlines the fact that the nation is its members – not necessarily those who occupy full citizenship status in the traditional sense but those who are resident within its borders. Here, Smith uses theatre to hold the nation to account. Marshalling a tragic moment in America's race relations as a microcosm of the multiple perspectives, lived experiences and attitudes to race and racial identity that the nation needs to contend with to move into the future, Smith shows a future not of agreement but of healthy disagreement, which lies at the heart of what it means to live in a diverse nation.

Nevertheless, the diversity of the nation is often masked by the unifying symbolic properties of national iconography – the focus of the next section.

National iconography

When we try to capture a nation in the mind's eye, that nation is often reduced to a constraining menu of icons that have, over time, come to stand in for the nation. Hence, stars and stripes, a dollar, the eagle, cowboys and Indians and the Statue of Liberty can signify the American nation. In imagining England, we might think of the Union Jack, Britannia, fish and chips, cups of tea, the bulldog, the red rose, the Queen and the Houses of Parliament. So, what purpose do these icons serve? They are a recognisable short-hand for the nation that symbolises something associated with the nation's history or cultural practices. In addition to suggesting symbolic membership of a national citizenry, icons are an important part of national branding and are intimately connected to the tourist and heritage industries. How better to mark a visit to France, say, than by buying a small replica of the Eiffel Tower, a string of onions and a jaunty beret?

However, it is important to stress that the meanings associated with national iconography do not stand still. There are frequent struggles over meaning and demands to rethink the status acquired or transmitted by national icons. In the United Kingdom, for instance, the association with football hooliganism and far-right politics taints the Union Jack and the Cross of St. George flags. And a mere sighting of one of these flags flying from a pub, house or car fills many of a left liberal disposition with unease about the overtures of imperial supremacy and right-wing political agendas that may or may not be implied. The connection between imperial power and national iconography is at the heart of John Osborne's state-of-the-nation play *The Entertainer* (Royal Court, London, 1957).

Theatre and national iconography: John Osborne's *The Entertainer*

The Entertainer uses the decline of the music hall as a central theatrical metaphor to explore what Osborne held to be the decline of the English nation, as he wrote in a note to the published play script: 'The music hall is dying, and, with it, a significant part of England.' Although Osborne makes clear that he is interested in the decline of England and a mythical sense of Englishness, the context he evokes is Britain's loss of empire and traditional values. For Osborne, it would seem, the nation as a viable entity is tied up in the success or failure of the modern nation-state on the world stage. Specifically, the (unnamed) Suez Crisis (1956) provides the real-life backdrop to the play. The political crisis in the Suez Canal region of Egypt followed intensive rearmament by Egypt, nationalisation of the Suez Canal and a plot by Egypt, Syria and Jordan to isolate Israel. After Israel launched a pre-emptive strike, the old colonial powers Britain and France requested all sides to withdraw and to agree to temporary occupation. When Egypt refused, Britain and France invaded the canal zone, only for the

USSR and the USA to force their withdrawal, an embarrassing public climb-down that finally sealed the deal on Britain's loss of power on the world stage. With these events in mind, Osborne frames a lament for the decline of empire, the presence of diasporic communities, shifting gender roles and the threats posed to the romantic Edwardian myth of traditional family values. In the play, the three generations of the Rice family serve as a 'national microcosm' (Kenneth Tynan, *Tynan on Theatre*, 1964, p. 49) exposing changing social values. However, their responses to the trajectory the nation are far from convergent.

The oldest member of the family, Billy, an elderly music hall entertainer, is effectively in mourning for an imperial past of unbesmirched British colonial rule and traditional gender roles. He sees his role as loudly bemoaning the state of the nation, whether that is manifest in the state of his beloved pint, the installation of a television in his local pub or the presence of foreigners in the boarding house where he lives. The youngest generation have an equally troubled, though different, relationship with the nation. Mick, Billy's grandson, is captured and killed while serving with the British army. Frank, his other grandson, is a conscientious objector who has spent time in prison for his refusal to fight for queen and country. And Jean, their sister, a fiercely independent young woman, acts on her ideological convictions when she attends a political protest rally against the occupation of the Suez canal in Trafalgar Square. Angry at and disenchanted with the nation in a totally dissimilar way to her grandfather, Jean repeatedly airs her frustrations at the older generation's adherence to a status quo of silent subservience to the monarchy, entrenched class relations and female subordination.

In the middle are the parents of Mick, Frank and Jean. Phoebe, their mother, numbs her existence with gin and easily forgettable movies, anaesthetising herself against Archie, her philandering husband, who faces a prison term for avoiding paying his taxes. Archie, played in the original production by Sir Laurence Olivier, is 'dead behind the eyes' and reduced to scraping by performing his tired music hall act as part of a nude review. He is morally and financially bankrupt, but he hides his failure and inability to communicate behind a rictus grin, slick patter and sexual promiscuity, and, like his wife, he is frequently reduced by alcohol to verbose sentimentalism and nostalgia. Archie stands in for contemporary England: he is shoddy and a failed performer, father, husband and citizen.

Throughout the play, Osborne hammers home his attack on the state of England by abusing national iconography to puncture any sense of national pride. In his jingoistic act, which punctuates the domestic scenes, Archie employs English iconography as a cheap trick to suggest a common bond with his audience – 'Look we're all English' – but Osborne cleverly turns the iconography on its head by associating it with a third-rate, unfunny act that speaks volumes about England's decline. As a Union Jack is unfurled on Archie's tawdry set, prompting a jingoistic song about 'Those bits of red still on the map/ We won't give up without a scrap' (p. 33), the whole British colonial project unravels

before the audience's eyes in the wake of postcolonial independence and the inept fiasco in Suez.

This iconographic imagery reaches its nadir when a
'spotlight behind gauze reveals a nude in Britannia's helmet
and holding a bulldog and trident' (p. 61) following a brief
extract from the patriotic song 'Land of Hope and Glory'.
Nude Britannia clutching a trident suggests the fragility of
the nation and its debasement; given Osborne's early support for the Campaign for Nuclear Disarmament (CND), it
might also suggest that the nation is sowing the seeds of its
own destruction.

English iconography reappears following the death
of Mick, whom the might of the British army failed to
protect – further evidence of England's disappointing
decline on the world stage. Before the funeral scene,
Frank sings a blues song about the return of Mick's body
to England that conjures up an image of a coffin draped
in the Union Jack, as is customary in such circumstances.
Like the earlier depiction of nude Britannia and trident,
this image conflates English iconography and death. A
young soldier's death is whitewashed by iconography that
suggests he died for a bigger and better cause, his nation.
This image echoes the concerns Billy expresses about the
cenotaph draped in flags that no longer commands the
respect it once did: 'If you took the flags off it I expect
they'd sit down and eat their sandwiches on it' (p. 79). It is
as if the only thing holding the nation together is its iconography, and Osborne shows this to be worn out, tainted
and hollow, a set of empty signifiers that have lost their

power and purpose. During the play, England is presented as being in its deaths throes, and when Billy, who metonymically stands in for the old 'glories' of imperial England and the music hall, dies, the final nails are hammered into his, and the nation's, Union Jack-covered coffin.

Unsettling iconography

During the 1990s, a concerted campaign to reclaim the Union Jack began as part of the 'Cool Britannia' marketing of Britain, which encompassed art, fashion, popular music and politics as New Labour marched triumphantly into power in 1997. In typically strident fashion, the Labour politician Peter Mandelson announced shortly afterwards,

> Now, together, we have reclaimed the flag. It is restored as an emblem of national pride and national diversity, restored from years as a symbol of division and intolerance to a symbol of confidence and unity for all the peoples and ethnic communities of a diverse and outward-looking Britain. (Quoted in Kevin Davey, *English Imaginaries: Six Studies in Anglo-British Modernity*, 1999, p. 11)

Well, that's all right then. Job done. In fact, the ideological complexities associated with the flag refused to go away, as Gordon Brown found out after urging the British people to 'fly the flag' for British identity and promoted 'British jobs for British workers' during his inaugural Labour conference speech as prime minister in 2007 in front of a large Union Jack backdrop. These words came back to haunt him in January 2009 when British workers, protesting at jobs going to European competitors, used the phrase on banners and placards. A phrase meant to be patriotically rousing in the context of a party political conference was branded by its critics as racist, illegal because it flouted European employment law, and protectionist.

Attention to the operations of national iconography in culture enables a fruitful discussion of the interplay of images and narratives in national identity formation. Cultural practices can bring forth the instabilities of national iconographies to question their potency, significance and signification. Indeed, the use and abuse of national iconography is a common strategy of cultural workers who want to challenge national iconography's institutional status, power and potential to exclude. This questioning inevitably entails a consideration of what falls outside as well as what falls inside national iconography. The exploration of absence as well as presence unmasks the sociopolitical divisions and power relations of gender, colonialism, class, race and sexuality inherent in national iconography.

For example, a recurring motif in the films and artworks produced by the queer artist Derek Jarman is the warping and distortion of national iconography. The cover image of his book *Kicking the Pricks* (1996) features a Union Jack with Jarman's disembodied head at its centre, an image recently reworked by Isaac Julien for his biopic, *Derek* (2008). In both images, Jarman confidently stares out at the viewer, staking his claim on and inserting himself into the most iconic of British insignia, the Union Jack, as if declaring, 'I am the nation too.' His queerness and HIV-positive status often placed him on the margins of the nation, so, for Jarman, national iconography offered a way of defying his nation to ignore his presence, his membership, his national citizenship.

In *The Entertainer* national iconography is used as a stick to beat England with – a petulant and rather lazy way of pointing to the nation's decline on the world stage. But recently theatre-makers and performance artists have deployed national iconography in far more ambiguous, playful, self-mocking and ambivalent ways. For example, a number have interrogated icons of national identity as a way of drawing attention to the slippage that occurs between projections of national identity and the complexities of lived experience in relation to regionalism, geographical displacement, exile, emigration and immigration. In *Anatomy of Two Exiles* by Desperate Optimists (Dartington College of Arts, UK, 1992) the Dublin-born artists Joe Lawlor and Christine Molloy, who choose to make work in England, played with narratives of national and individual identity through personal memories, story-telling, confessions, records, dances and visual signifiers. Filling the performance space with cultural signifiers of or associated with Irishness, such as national dress, Guinness, a crucifix, a statue of the Virgin Mary, a balaclava, potatoes, a clod of earth and Irish dancing, the company disturbed the seemingly easy relationship between these cultural signifiers of national identity and the representation of an authentic, stable and unified self.

Similarly, Third Angel created a participatory project called *Pleasant Land* (Leeds Metropolitan University Gallery, 2003), an explicit reference to William Blake's patriotic and romantic take on England in his rousing work 'Jerusalem'. Probing beneath the surface of this patriotic imagining of the nation, Third Angel invited people to submit postcards, stories, images, objects and declarations on their England and Englishness, which the company assembled on a website and as part of an installation. *Pleasant Land's* polyvocality emphasised the multiplicity of Englishnesses: it is rural and urban, seaside and city centre, terraced houses and castles, polite and aggressive, the stiff upper lip and vocal/physical expressiveness, slightly embarrassing and something to celebrate.

With his group La Pocha Nostra, Guillermo Gómez-Peña has created numerous interactive performances, including *Temple of Confessions* (Scottsdale Centre for the Arts, Arizona, 1994) and *Ex-Centris* (Tate Modern, London, 2003), that rely heavily on the presentation, re-framing and collision of national and religious icons to engage performatively with questions of political power, the legacy of colonialism and the creation of fetishised national stereotypes. Born in Mexico, living between Mexico and the United States and making performance works throughout the world, Gómez-Peña is interested in the territory between and across national boundaries – what he refers to as 'border cultures'. Playing with the aesthetics of ethnographic display and cultural dioramas, Gómez-Peña explores fears of the racial, sexual and cultural *other* by warping and blurring cultural iconography and challenging spectators to look afresh at the meanings they associate with these signifiers.

These performance examples celebrate hybridity and embrace the plurality of identities that co-exist in and between nations, a theme echoed in *Flag Metamorphoses* (2006), a video installation curated by Myrian Thymes. Commissioned in 2005 by the Swiss Federal Office of Culture, *Flag Metamorphoses* involved artists and filmmakers from around the world, including the United States, Germany, Denmark, Croatia and the United Kingdom. The installation, first shown in March 2006 at the AniMOweb Festival in Modena, Italy, has subsequently toured to festivals and exhibitions in Los Angeles, Melbourne, Vienna, Madrid and Manchester, among other places.

The piece presents a mosaic of national interconnectivity through Flash animation that slowly transforms two or more national flags into each other via other imagery and aural signifiers. Each animation explores shared histories, territories, cultural practices, antagonisms, rituals, religion, diaspora, musical affinities, political battles and trade relations, and the work encompasses subjects as diverse as the Cuban Missile Crisis, football, the myths of 'fair trade', colonialism and the postcolonial legacy, the Balkan conflict and the Amazon rainforest. For example, the UK-based artist Rona Innes morphs the Indian flag into the Scottish flag via sitar music and Highland bagpipes, with images of crops, transportation, the sea, industry and jute fibres, with a view to animating the following passage:

> Jute has been grown in the Indian subcontinent for centuries. In 1793, the Bengal Board of Trade sent a jute fibre sample to Great Britain. Starting [in]1833, jute fibre was spun mechanically in Dundee, Scotland. Dundee had the advantage of locally supplied whale oil to make the jute fibres flexible and a workforce of women experienced in the spinning and weaving of linen. Scotland's jute prosperity was to last for over 100 years, until India developed the capacity to manufacture and process the raw material. (www.flag-metamorphoses.net)

Behind this simple description and Flash animation lies a complex history of colonialism, the Industrial Revolution, gender roles, the exploitation of natural resources, the status of developing nations and global trade. *Flag Metamorphoses* highlights how any one nation is engaged in many political, economic and cultural exchanges, and it problematises the supposed flattening out of nations associated with globalisation. Emphasising the spaces between nations, *Flag Metamorphoses* destabilises any focus on the nation as a singular, homogeneous entity hermetically sealed from wider global relations. Nations are seen to be interdependent and in constant flux. By blurring and re-visioning national flags, this art project reassesses the supposed fixity of national iconography and suggests that national identities and the relations between nations are never static but are in a constant process of reappraisal and renewal. In fact, the piece emphasises how nations stay functional through this permanent re-creation of values, symbols and relations.

This stress on plurality and the cross-cultural relationships between and within nations drives the focus of the next section.

Cosmopolitanism: beyond the nation

In this section I search for instances of what we might call a 'convivial theatre'. I am deliberately using 'convivial' as an allied term of the more popular 'cosmopolitanism', which has been prominent in theoretical and cultural discourse in recent years, and I should take some time to explain why I find 'conviviality' a useful term, even though the two are inextricably linked.

Cosmopolitanism can be traced back to the Stoics of ancient Greece and Rome and to key thinkers such as Dante Alighieri and Immanuel Kant, who promoted the desirability of an international government. The term is not consistently applied, and many have modified its universalising tendencies to make it speak to and for their areas of concern (Helen Gilbert and Jacqueline Lo, *Performance and Cosmopolitics*, 2007, pp. 4–6; Paul Rae, 'Where Is the Cosmopolitan Stage?', 2006, p. 10), but, broadly speaking, there is a common agenda. At the heart of cosmopolitanism's popularity is the sense that it acknowledges cultural, religious and national difference, for example, while recognising simultaneously a layer of shared moral imperatives that unite people throughout the world. This perspective is enshrined in institutions such as the United Nations and is the principle behind the Universal Declaration of Human Rights. Thus, cosmopolitanism invites us to think of citizens of the world, of global citizens, alongside identities more locally specific to geographical placement or individual subjectivities. Cosmopolitanism is about sharing the same planet and recognising the ethical obligations of healthy co-existence that this demands.

For many scholars, theatre and performance offers a potential site for cosmopolitanism because it involves human beings in shared time and space. Thus, in *Theatre & the City* (2009), Harvie writes about 'that extraordinary (ordinary) performative experience of feeling like a community in an audience one feels very different from' in terms of age, class, geographical region and ethnicity, and she suggests that some theorists would call this a 'cosmopolitan' experience (p. 76). Paul Rae argues, in 'Where Is the Cosmopolitan Stage?', that cosmopolitanism is central to 'an experience of theatrical spatiality that expresses the intertwined experiences of place and identity in an age of complex global connectivity' (pp. 10–11), and in *Theatre & Globalization*, Dan Rebellato suggests that 'the theatre's formal modes tend towards cosmopolitanism' (p. 75). For a concrete example of this in practice we may think of Complicite's *A Disappearing Number* (Plymouth Theatre Royal, 2007), which explores love, loss and the nature of understanding across histories and three continents. Emphasising the interconnectivity of people, places and ideas, the production was deeply cosmopolitan in its enquiry, narrative and theatrical telling, which used gauzes and new technologies to move seamlessly across time and space.

Cosmopolitanism and nationalism

The transnational quality of cosmopolitanism has led some thinkers to perceive the relationship between cosmo-politanism and nationalism as fraught, largely because there is an implication that nations have to give up a degree of national sovereignty and autonomy to participate fully in a cosmopolitan community. Arguably, the French Revolution provided one of the defining challenges to the cosmopolitan ethos that underpinned much Enlightenment thinking of the eighteenth century. According to Daniele Conversi, in 'Cosmopolitanism and Nationalism' (2001), Maximilien Robespierre, a French lawyer, politician and key figure of the French Revolution, 'interpreted cosmopolitan ideas about the universal rights of man quite selectively, emphasizing them only when they coincided with his view of the national interest' (p. 35). The glorification of modern nationalism ignited by the French Revolution held sway throughout the nineteenth and twentieth centuries and placed the very idea of cosmopolitanism under strain as national interest con-sistently trumped the cosmopolitan ideal.

Nonetheless, cosmopolitanism has regained currency in recent years as a means of articulating the implica-tions of living in an increasingly globalised world. And, as we proceed through the twenty-first century, it would seem that the way to embrace nationalism, difference and cosmopolitanism positively has become a primary item on the political agenda. This was epitomised by Barack Obama's inaugural speech in 2009 when he declared,

> We are a nation of Christians and Muslims, Jews and Hindus – and non-believers. We are shaped by every language and culture, drawn from every end of this Earth; and because we have tasted the bitter swill of civil war and segregation, and emerged from that dark chapter stronger and more united, we cannot help but believe that the old hatreds shall someday pass; that the lines of tribe shall soon dissolve; that as the world grows smaller, our common humanity shall reveal itself. (http://www.timesonline.co.uk/tol/news/world/us_and_americas/us_elections/article5554819.ece)

Cosmopolitanism under threat

In *After Empire*, Paul Gilroy suggests that 'the meaning and ambition of the term "cosmopolitanism" has been hijacked and diminished' (p. 66) by the recast global conditions of the 'war on terror', panic about asylum-seekers and fear of Muslim orchestrated terrorism. He writes that 'the desire to presume the equal worth of alien cultures and to offer equal respect in proliferating encounters with otherness is thought to be misguided or out of date' (p. 65). For Gilroy, the nation-state is, once again, strengthened by the priority attached to national security, enforcing national borders and evicting nationals and non-nationals who pose a threat to the national fabric. For him, in campaigns such as the Iraq War, cosmopolitanism is tainted by a neo-imperial agenda:

> In the names of cosmopolitanism and humani-
> tarianism, these particular moral sensibilities
> can promote and justify intervention in other
> people's sovereign territory on the grounds that
> their ailing or incompetent national state has
> failed to measure up to the levels of good prac-
> tice that merit recognition as civilized. (p. 66)

Importantly, his aim is not to undermine the original Enlightenment intention of world citizenship but to suggest that the term 'cosmopolitanism' has been hijacked by a 'brand of ethical imperialism' (p. 69) that attempts to form a coalition of willing national states to fight for the *universal* human rights associated with the spread of liberal democracy and capitalism. As an alternative, Gilroy suggests that there is potential in what he refers to as a more 'vulgar' or 'demotic' cosmopolitanism. To this end, Gilroy offers up the possibility of *conviviality* as a way of extending and strengthening the application of multicultural and cosmopolitan ideals in daily life and cultural practice.

Cosmopolitan conviviality

Gilroy claims conviviality could act as a therapeutic counter to the collective melancholia afflicting Britain in the wake of its imperial history, turbulent race relations and current cultural crisis around what 'Englishness' and 'Britishness' mean as a result of immigration and the presence of second- and third-generation 'native' national citizens born in Britain. But I think we can use the term beyond Gilroy's focus on racial difference and the British experience. The predominant *civic* and *ethnic* versions of the nation, in emphasising the workings of the state or the sustenance of a pure ethnic ancestral heritage, pay little heed to the ways that people, who inhabit and make up nations, func- tion day to day through meetings, interactions and collab- orations across national boundaries and ethnic cultures. At this level of national daily life, Gilroy's emphasis on con- viviality becomes useful. He argues that the term enables a move away from the focus on identity and that 'the rad- ical openness that brings conviviality alive makes a nonsense of closed, fixed, and reified identity and turns attention toward the always-unpredictable mechanisms of identifica- tion' (*After Empire*, p. xi). Hence, the focus on identity – for our purposes, national identity – is destabilised, and instead cultural practices arising out of cohabitation and interaction take on primary significance.

In contrast to cosmopolitanism, which stresses universal rights, global co-existence and a sense of common human- ity, conviviality potentially offers a view of the nation that is not about eradicating hostility or antagonism but about being open to them and providing spaces for debate, dis- sent and a coming together of multiple perspectives and modes of being and behaving. The way conviviality sug- gests other terms such as 'inclusiveness', 'hospitality' and 'sociability' places greater emphasis on encounters between different people. It is not just a respectful recognition of the moral obligations that global citizenship opens up; it is about embracing rather than hiding away from or ignoring the messy, conflict-ridden aspects of diversity of races, cultures, religions, sexualities, classes, ages and national identifications.

So, what might convivial culture encompass? According to Gilroy, it is marked by its unruliness, a haphazard quality whereby literature, art and above all popular culture are capable of generating 'emancipatory interruptions' through moments of clash and rupture. Theatre, in particular, can have an important role here. Gilroy writes that convivial culture 'glories in the ordinary virtues and ironies – listening, looking, discretion, friendship – that can be cultivated when mundane encounters with difference become rewarding' (*After Empire*, p. 75). I would argue that theatre, like music (from which Gilroy draws many of his examples), provides a heightened space where people come together to create work that relies on the collision and integration of different perspectives and skills and that the qualities of listening, looking and responsiveness are highly regarded activities in both making and watching theatre.

Convivial theatre

There are two examples I want to use of what a convivial theatre might entail, look like and feel like for an audience. The first is *The Theft of Sita* (Adelaide Festival, 2000), a collaboration between Australian and Indonesian performers;

the second is the British sculptor Antony Gormley's 2009 work *One and Other* (Trafalgar Square, London).

To create *The Theft of Sita*, the director Nigel Jamieson and composer Paul Grabowsky brought together twenty-four independent artists and technicians, including musicians and puppeteers from Indonesia and Australia, and the British designer Julian Crouch. The making of the work involved cross-cultural collaboration and acute sensitivity to national circumstances and cultural practices. *The Theft of Sita* was created during a period of intense political turmoil following the removal of the Indonesian leader Suharto from office in 1998 after mass protests about corruption and human rights abuses. The company began work in November 1999, at the height of the tensions surrounding the appointment of Suharto's successor and the future of East Timor, which was fighting to gain independence as a nation after twenty-five years of Indonesian occupation. These political tensions led to the resignation of the original *dalang* (puppet master), I Wayan Wija, from the project, but the rest of the company continued under fraught circumstances. I Made Sidia replaced Wayan as puppet master early in 2000, but when he arrived in Adelaide, Australian custom officers confiscated his puppets, traditionally believed to be imbued with the power of the gods, and gassed them with insecticide. As Jamieson ironically commented, 'Australians are very big on foreign pests' (quoted in Paul Taylor, 'The Theft of Sita', 2001, p. 15).

Despite difficulties rooted in specific national circumstances and anxieties, cosmopolitan conviviality won out,

and the artists collaborated by listening to and experi-
menting with each other. This convivial approach is best
illustrated by the way *The Theft of Sita* cross-pollinated the
musical forms of Balinese gamelan and jazz:

> The former is tuned according to completely
> different principles to Western instruments, and
> the result was cacophony. The problem was over-
> come by a day of intense mutual listening – a
> model, says Jamieson, of cultures adjusting to
> each other. (Quoted in Taylor, 'The Theft of
> Sita', p. 15)

The whole production worked through a process of developing understanding, accommodations and transformations. It
combined live music and traditional shadow puppetry with
video animation, computer-generated images and photo-
graphic documentation projected onto giant screens. When
I saw the show at the Warwick Arts Centre in 2001, this
combination offered a striking example of how the old and
the new, the traditional and the contemporary, the cultur-
ally specific and the universally applicable could co-exist in
fruitful collaboration. This was equally true of the narrative
structure, which spoke to and of the local (national) situation in Indonesia and the global (transnational) situation in
terms of the impact of environmental destruction, rampant
tourism and unrestrained market forces.

Based on the ancient love story of Sita and Rama from
the Sanskrit epic the *Ramayana*, and set after the demon

Rahwana has abducted Sita and carried her off to his kingdom of Langka, *The Theft of Sita* exploded into new territory. In this version, the father and son Tualen and Merdah rescue Sita, but not before they witness huge logging machines embark on deforestation as the beautiful, lush landscape is made a haven for tourists and Langka is transformed into a gleaming metropolis of high-rise temples to commerce and the leisure industry. With careful splicing of footage documenting the recent popular protest movement in Indonesia, Sita's rescue was equated with the overthrow of Suharto, and the potential for a new dawn in the region was signalled by Tualen and Merdah 'hovering nervously at the ballot box' (Taylor, 'The Theft of Sita', p. 15).

In many ways, the creative impetus and process that generated *The Theft of Sita* offered a model of conviviality in the complex negotiation of the difficulties of cultural encounters across nations, narratives and theatrical traditions. And the attentive dialogue that enabled this production to come about continued as it toured Germany, New York and London on the international festival circuit. This production was about a nation, Indonesia, but it was made possible only through collaboration and the money made available through the high-profile international touring network. Although international festivals are often accused of encouraging bland homogenisation, I would argue that this was far from the case with *The Theft of Sita* because it maintained its faith in the potential of a traditional story and story-telling in creative collision with new modes and stories.

In contrast to the interlacing of national and international concerns in *The Theft of Sita*, Gormley claimed his one-hundred-day public art project *One and Other*, begun on 6 July 2009, was about 'creating a picture of Britain, and we don't yet know what that picture in composite will be' (Charlotte Higgins, 'On Culture Blog', 2009, p. 1). Gormley's work explores the body and its relationship to public space, memory, history, the collective body and the environment. He normally casts sculptures of bodies in hard materials such as bronze, iron and stainless steel, but *One and Other* used the live human form. Commissioned by the mayor of London and produced by Artichoke, the creative organisation behind such large-scale public events as La Machine's fifty-foot spider, *La Princesse* (Liverpool City, 2008), and Royal de Luxe's visit to London with *The Sultan's Elephant* (Nantes, 2005), this was another form of intervention in the cityscape. The piece involved members of the public applying to spend an hour on the empty fourth plinth in London's Trafalgar Square. Since 1998, the fourth plinth, originally designed by Sir Charles Barry and built in 1841 to display an equestrian statue that never materialised, has been used to house temporary artworks, including works by the artists Marc Quinn and Rachel Whiteread.

Gormley decided to give this public space in the heart of London over to the nation by choosing 2,400 participants, with an equal gender split, who represented every region of the United Kingdom, from the tens of thousands of people who applied to be part of the artwork. Anyone over sixteen could apply to go on the plinth; those who were selected could decide exactly how they used the time and space. In a work designed to democratise art and public space, Gormley wanted to replace the political, military and royal figures who traditionally occupy the plinths in Trafalgar Square with ordinary citizens. He explained his rationale in the following terms:

> In the context of Trafalgar Square with its milit-
> ary, valedictory and male historical statues, this
> elevation of everyday life to the position formerly
> occupied by monumental art allows us to reflect
> on the diversity, vulnerability and particular-
> ity of the individual in contemporary society.
> (www.antonygormley.com)

Rather than presenting a homogeneous picture of the nation, Gormley invited a rampant polyvocality. The project utilised a literal raised platform where people claimed a space and a vehicle to express themselves, their views and their concerns. It provided an inclusive, non-judgemental space on which 2,400 people staked their claim for what they wanted the nation to see, hear and encounter. Technology made the project available to a wide audience through live twenty-four-hour web streaming and a weekly round-up on the Sky Arts channel. As living artworks, participants used their hour to dance, to read, to play instruments and to hula-hoop. They deployed bubbles, balloons, placards, loud hailers and costumes. Some approached their hour in silence; others used the hour to promote themselves, a product or a cause or to protest against issues such as the war in Afghanistan, the British National Party, climate change, the cancellation of a language course at Imperial College London, female genital mutilation and homelessness. The project moved between modes and concerns that embodied the personal and the political, the introvert and the extrovert, the local and the global, the national and the international, the low tech and the high tech, and the playful and the serious. In the sum of the 2,400 parts, Gormley created a unique composite, a snapshot of the nation – but one underlined by the fact that given another 2,400 participants the picture would have been completely different.

Conclusion

In *One and Other*, Gormley did not try to impose his version of what should occupy a national monument at the heart of England's capital, beyond a concern to see a broad cross-section of 'ordinary' citizens represented. He did not dictate, beyond demanding equal gender and regional representation, who should have a national platform. He did not try to assert a national narrative or agenda. Gormley convivially opened a platform for national citizens diverse in age, race, culture, gender, sexuality and regional affiliation to express themselves as individuals and also, as the title of the piece suggests, in relation to each other. They cohabited the fourth plinth, and the eclectic picture that emerged highlights the impossibility of unifying the national image. Moreover, the various audiences for this piece – including friends and relatives of participants, passers-by, tourists and those watching Sky Arts or browsing the Internet – relied on the nexus of personal and geographical interconnectivity that exists in the contemporary world. At the same time, Gormley framed his rationale for the project as wanting to provide a composite image, a 'portrait of the UK now', that revealed issues, concerns and, above all, 'what we care about' (www.oneandother.co.uk). In summoning the 'we' of the nation, Gormley revealed the doggedness of the nation and national identity as an organising principle. A desire to know who 'we' are has galvanised much of the theatre practice discussed in this book, and the question remains as persistent as ever, as *One and Other* demonstrates. The impossibility of answering the question provides fertile material for theatre practitioners.

I hope I have shown that as nations continue to evolve in response to internal changes and global circumstances, the narratives and modes that represent aspects of the nation will grow and proliferate. International exchange and new media technologies will encourage and enable increasing transnational cooperation and creativity that will continue irrevocably to influence and alter national cultural practices. Theatre can and will continue to hold a mirror up to the nation, but this does not mean that the mirror has to reflect an accurate picture – it can be distorted, expansive and utopian. Or it can reflect as many different versions of the nation as there are people, as *One and Other* demonstrates. Theatre has the potential not just to reflect what is happening in a nation at any given time but, via its discursive, imaginative and communal realm, to contribute to the creation of the nation through the cultural discourses it ignites, the representations it offers and the stories it chooses to tell. However, if we take Gilroy at his word, then theatre that engages with the nation will have to move away from tired and impossible questions of national identity and instead rely on creative interactions and collaborations that continually make and re-make the nation in the present tense.

further reading

There are numerous books on the nation and nationalism, but the important work of Anthony D. Smith should be the first point of call for anyone who wants to understand the complexities of the subject. In particular, I recommend his book *Nationalism*, from Polity's key concepts series, as an excellent introduction to the topic. I also find David McCrone's *The Sociology of Nationalism* useful and provocative. For a historical approach, take a look at Hobsbawm's *Nations and Nationalism since 1780: Programme, Myth, Reality*. In *Nationalism: A Very Short Introduction*, Steven Grosby tackles the relationship between history, religion, culture and nations. Homi K. Bhabha's *Nation and Narration* and Gopal Balakrishnan's *Mapping the Nation* are wide-ranging and remarkably useful collections of essays that take different approaches to the topic. Benedict Anderson's *Imagined Communities* has been so incredibly influential that it is impossible to ignore. For studies on the relationship between race and nation, you cannot beat the work of Paul Gilroy, who always offers a challenging and engaging read.

Most books that deal with theatre and the nation focus on a particular geographical region; see, for example, the works listed below by Joanne Tompkins on Australia, Aparna Bhargava Dharwadker on India, S. E. Wilmer on America, Ben Levitas on Ireland and Jen Harvie on the United Kingdom. Kiki Gounaridou has edited a strong collection of essays on different national contexts. These are all great books that offer fascinating insights into the subject. Loren Kruger, S. E. Wilmer and Laurence Senelick deal with the historical and contemporary role of official national theatres in Europe and America. In his essay 'From the State of the Nation to Globalization', Dan Rebellato looks at the move away from the state-of-the-nation play, and his *Theatre & Globalization* – in this series – is an engaging place to gather ideas about the impact of globalisation on theatre, as is Harvie and Rebellato's special issue of *Contemporary Theatre Review* 16.1 (2006) on the same subject.

Agnès, Catherine Poirier. 'You Crazy Rosbifs.' *Guardian* 12 April 2005. 27 May 2009 <www.guardian.co.uk/books/2005/apr/12/britishidentity.society>.

Anderson, Benedict. *Imagined Communities.* 2nd edition. London: Verso, 2006.

Balakrishnan, Gopal, ed. *Mapping the Nation.* London: Verso, 1996.

Benhabib, Seyla. *Another Cosmopolitanism.* Ed. Robert Post. Oxford: Oxford UP, 2008.

Bhabha, Homi K., ed. *Nation and Narration.* London: Routledge, 1990.

Bharucha, Rustom. *The Politics of Cultural Practice: Thinking Through Theatre in an Age of Globalization.* London: Athlone, 2000.

Billig, Michael. *Banal Nationalism*. London: Sage, 1995.

Billington, Michael. *State of the Nation: British Theatre since 1945*. London: Faber & Faber, 2007.

Breuilly, John. *Nationalism and the State*. 2nd edition. Manchester: Manchester UP, 1993.

Brown, Mark. 'Wales Raises Curtain on £3m National Theatre.' *Guardian* 5 November 2009: 6.

Carlson, Marvin. 'National Theatres: Then and Now.' *National Theatres in a Changing Europe*. Ed. S. E. Wilmer. Basingstoke, UK: Palgrave Macmillan, 2008. 21–33.

Chatterjee, Partha. 'Whose Imagined Community?' *Mapping the Nation*. Ed. Gopal Balakrishnan. London: Verso, 1996. 214–25.

Chatterjee, Sudipto. 'The Nation Staged: Nationalist Discourse in Late 19th Century Bengali Theatre.' *Modern Indian Theatre: A Reader*. Ed. Nandi Bhatia. Oxford: Oxford UP, 2009. 97–131.

Chaudhuri, Una. 'Theatre and Cosmopolitanism: New Stories, Old Stages.' *Cosmopolitan Geographies: New Locations in Literature and Culture*. Ed. Vinay Dharwadker. New York: Routledge, 2000. 171–95.

Conversi, Daniele. 'Cosmopolitanism and Nationalism.' *Encyclopaedia of Nationalism*. Ed. Athena S. Leoussi. New Brunswick and London: Transaction, 2001. 34–39.

Davey, Kevin. *English Imaginaries: Six Studies in Anglo-British Modernity*. London: Lawrence & Wishart, 1999.

Dharwadker, Aparna Bhargava. *Theatres of Independence: Drama, Theory and Urban Performance in India since 1947*. Iowa City: U of Iowa P, 2005.

Dolan, Jill. *Utopia in Performance: Finding Hope at the Theater*. Ann Arbor: U of Michigan P, 2005.

Easthope, Antony. *Englishness and National Culture*. London: Routledge, 1999.

Eriksen, Thomas Hylland, and Richard Jenkins, eds. *Flag, Nation and Symbolism in Europe and America*. Abingdon, UK: Routledge, 2007.

Fanon, Frantz. *Black Skin, White Masks*. New York: Grove, 1968.

Fourie, Charles J. *New South African Plays*. London: Aurora Metro, 2006.

Gellner, Ernest. *Nations and Nationalism*. 2nd edition. Oxford: Blackwell, 2006.

Gilbert, Helen, and Jacqueline Lo. *Performance and Cosmopolitics: Cross-Cultural Transactions in Australasia*. Basingstoke, UK: Palgrave Macmillan, 2007.

Gilroy, Paul. *There Ain't No Black in the Union Jack: The Cultural Politics of Race and Nation*. London: Routledge, 1987.

————. *After Empire: Melancholia or Convivial Culture?* Abingdon, UK: Routledge, 2004.

Gounaridou, Kiki, ed. *Staging Nationalism: Essays on Theatre and National Identity*. Jefferson, NC: McFarland, 2005.

Grogan, Molly. 'Theater Director Mohamed Rouabhi's France.' n.d. 5 March 2010 <www.parisvoice.com/index.php?option=com_content&task=view&id=486&Itemid=35>.

Grosby, Steven. *Nationalism: A Very Short Introduction*. Oxford: Oxford UP, 2005.

Hall, Stuart. 'Whose Heritage? Un-settling 'the Heritage', Reimagining the Post-nation.' *The Politics of Heritage: The Legacies of 'Race'*. Ed. Jo Littler and Roshi Naidoo. London: Routledge, 2005. 23–35.

Harvie, Jen. *Staging the UK*. Manchester: Manchester UP, 2005.

————. *Theatre & the City*. Basingstoke, UK: Palgrave Macmillan, 2009.

Harvie, Jen, and Dan Rebellato, eds. *Globalisation and Theatre*. Spec. iss. of *Contemporary Theatre Review* 16.1 (2006).

Higgins, Charlotte. 'On Culture Blog,' 6 July 2009. 22 March 2010 <www.guardian.co.uk/culture/charlottehigginsblog/2009/jul/06/fourth-plinth-protest>.

Hobsbawm, Eric. 'Introduction: Inventing Traditions.' *The Invention of Tradition*. Ed. Eric Hobsbawm and Terence Ranger. Cambridge: Cambridge UP, 1983. 1–14.

————. 'Waving Flags: Nations and Nationalism.' *The Age of Empire 1875–1914*. London: Weidenfeld & Nicolson, 1987. 142–64.

————. *Nations and Nationalism since 1780: Programme, Myth, Reality*. Cambridge: Cambridge UP, 1990.

Holmwood, Leigh. 'Susan Boyle: A Dream Come True.' *Guardian* 18 April 2009. 27 May 2009 <www.guardian.co.uk/media/2009/apr/18/susan-boyle-britains-got-talent>.

Hutchinson, John, and Anthony D. Smith. *Nationalism*. Oxford: Oxford UP, 1994.

Jarman, Derek. *Kicking the Pricks*. London: Vintage, 1996.

Jones, Anwen. *National Theatres in Context: France, Germany, England and Wales*. Cardiff: U of Wales P, 2007.

Klaic, Dragan. 'National Theatres Undermined by the Withering of the Nation-State.' *National Theatres in a Changing Europe*. Ed. S. E. Wilmer. Basingstoke, UK: Palgrave Macmillan, 2008. 217–27.

Kohn, Hans. *The Idea of Nationalism*. 2nd edition. New York: Collier-Macmillan, 1967.

Kruger, Loren. *The National Stage: Theatre and Cultural Legitimation in England, France and America*. Chicago, IL: U of Chicago P, 1992.

———. 'The National Stage and the Naturalized House: (Trans)National Legitimation in Modern Europe.' *National Theatres in a Changing Europe*. Ed. S. E. Wilmer. Basingstoke, UK: Palgrave Macmillan, 2008. 34–48.

Kymlicka, Will. 'Liberal Nationalism and Cosmopolitan Justice.' *Another Cosmopolitanism*. Ed. Robert Post. Oxford: Oxford UP, 2008. 128–44.

Levitas, Ben. *The Theatre of Nation: Irish Drama and Cultural Nationalism 1880–1916*. Oxford: Oxford UP, 2002.

Martin, Carol. 'Bearing Witness: Anna Deavere Smith from Community to Theatre to Mass Media.' *A Sourcebook of Feminist Theatre and Performance*. Ed. Carol Martin. London and New York: Routledge, 1996. 81–93.

McConachie, Bruce. 'Towards a History of National Theatres in Europe.' *National Theatres in a Changing Europe*. Ed. S. E. Wilmer. Basingstoke, UK: Palgrave Macmillan, 2008. 49–60.

McCrone, David. *The Sociology of Nationalism*. London: Routledge, 1998.

Mouffe, Chantal, ed. *Dimensions of Radical Democracy: Pluralism, Citizenship, Community*. London: Verso, 1992.

Osborne, John. *The Entertainer*. London: Faber & Faber, 1957.

Perryman, Mark, ed. *Imagined Nation: England after Britain*. London: Lawrence & Wishart, 2008.

Rae, Paul. 'Where Is the Cosmopolitan Stage?' *Contemporary Theatre Review* 16.1 (2006): 8–22.

Rebellato, Dan. 'From the State of the Nation to Globalization: Shifting Political Agendas in Contemporary British Playwriting.' *A Concise Companion to British and Irish Drama*. Ed. Nadine Holdsworth and Mary Luckhurst. Oxford: Blackwell, 2008. 245–62.

———. *Theatre & Globalization*. Basingstoke, UK: Palgrave Macmillan, 2009.

Reinelt, Janelle. 'Notes for a Radical Democratic Theater: Productive Crises and the Challenge of Indeterminacy.' *Staging Resistance: Essays on Political Theater*. Ed. Jeanne Colleran and Jenny S. Spencer. Michigan: U of Michigan P, 1998. 283–300.

Reinelt, Janelle. 'The Role of National Theatres in the Age of Globalization.' *National Theatres in a Changing Europe*. Ed. S. E. Wilmer. Basingstoke, UK: Palgrave Macmillan, 2008. 228–38.

Renan, Ernest. 'What Is a Nation?' *Nation and Narration*. Ed. Homi K. Bhabha. London: Routledge, 1990. 8–22.

Reynolds, Larry J. 'American Cultural Iconography.' *National Imaginaries, American Identities: The Cultural Work of American Iconography*. Ed. Larry J. Reynolds and Gordon Hutner. Princeton, NJ: Princeton UP, 2000. 3–28.

Richards, Sandra, L. 'Caught in the Act of Social Definition: *On the Road* with Anna Deavere Smith.' *Acting Out: Feminist Performances*. Ed. Lynda Hart and Peggy Phelan. Michigan: U of Michigan P, 1993. 35–53.

Robinson, James, and Leigh Holmwood. 'BBC Kills Off Robin Hood as Viewing Figures Fall.' *Guardian* 2 July 2009. 28 July 2009 <www.guardian.co.uk/media/2009/jul/02/robin-hood-bbc-tv-drama>.

Senelick, Laurence, ed. *National Theatre in Northern and Eastern Europe 1746–1900*. Cambridge: Cambridge UP, 1991.

Smith, Anna Deavere. *Fires in the Mirror: Crown Heights, Brooklyn and Other Identities*. New York: Dramatists Play Service, 1993.

Smith, Anthony D. *Nationalism*. Cambridge: Polity, 2001.

Taylor, Paul. 'The Theft of Sita: A New Wizard of Oz.' *Independent* 24 October 2001: p. 15.

Tompkins, Joanne. *Unsettling Space: Contestations in Contemporary Australian Theatre*. Basingstoke, UK: Palgrave Macmillan, 2006.

Tynan, Kenneth. *Tynan on Theatre*. Harmondsworth, UK: Penguin, 1964.

Walker, Tim. 'Cowell's Reality Circus Espouses British Talent for Eccentricity.' *Independent* 26 May 2009. 27 May 2009 <www.independent.co.uk/opinion/commentators/tim-walker-cowells-reality-circus-espouses-british-talent-for-eccentricity-1690629.html>.

Williams, Roy. *Sing Yer Heart Out for the Lads. Plays: 2*. London: Methuen, 2004.

Wilmer, S. E., *Theatre, Society and Nation*. Cambridge: Cambridge UP, 2002.

———— ed. *Writing and Rewriting National Theatre Histories*. Iowa City: U of Iowa P, 2004.

———— ed. *National Theatres in a Changing Europe*. Basingstoke, UK: Palgrave Macmillan, 2008.

index

acknowledgements

I would like to thank series editor Dan Rebellato for his insight and sensitive comments on early drafts of this book, and Kate Haines at Palgrave Macmillan for her advice and patience. I am grateful to my colleagues, especially to Milija Gluhovic, Yvette Hutchison and Janelle Reinelt, for their help and to Shamsiya Qasim for alerting me to the theatrical climate in Tajikistan.

My love and thanks, as ever, to Geoff and Corin.

Theatre& small books on theatre & everything else

NEW FOR 2010...

978-0-230-57548-6

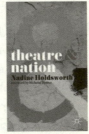

978-0-230-21871-0

978-0-230-57462-5

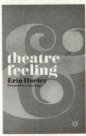

978-0-230-21846-8

978-0-230-22064-5

'Palgrave Macmillan's excellent new outward-looking, eclectic *Theatre&* series. These short books, written by leading theatre academics, do much to reintroduce some of the brightest names in theatre academia to the general reader.' - Guardian Theatre blog

Theatre& small books on theatre & everything else

PUBLISHED IN 2009...

978-0-230-20522-2

978-0-230-20523-9

978-0-230-20524-6

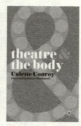
978-0-230-20543-7

> 'Short, sharp shots' for theatre students and enthusiasts
> Presenting the best writing from A-list scholars
> Vibrant and inspiring

978-0-230-21028-8

978-0-230-21830-7

978-0-230-21027-1

978-0-230-21857-4

Place your order online at www.palgrave.com